# From periphery to centre

## Domestic violence in work with abused children

Marianne Hester and Chris Pearson

The POLICY
PRESS

First published in Great Britain in 1998 by

The Policy Press
University of Bristol
Rodney Lodge
Grange Road
Bristol BS8 4EA
UK

Tel     +44 (0)117 973 8797
Fax     +44 (0)117 973 7308
E-mail   tpp@bristol.ac.uk
http://www.bristol.ac.uk/Publications/TPP/

© The Policy Press and the Joseph Rowntree Foundation, 1998

In association with the Joseph Rowntree Foundation

ISBN 1 86134 115 6

**Marianne Hester** is and **Chris Pearson** was until recently based in the Domestic Violence Research Group, University of Bristol.

The **Joseph Rowntree Foundation** has supported this project as part of its programme of research and innovative development projects, which it hopes will be of value to policy makers and practitioners. The facts presented and the views expressed in this report, however, are those of the authors and not necessarily those of the Foundation.

The statements and opinions contained within this publication are solely those of the authors and contributors and not of The University of Bristol or The Policy Press. The University of Bristol and The Policy Press disclaim responsibility for any injury to persons or property resulting from any material published in this publication.

The Policy Press works to counter discrimination on grounds of gender, race, disability, age and sexuality.

Cover design by Qube Design Associates, Bristol.
Printed in Great Britain by Hobbs the Printers Ltd, Southampton.

# Contents

# Acknowledgements

We want to thank everyone who contributed to the research. The research was supported by a grant from the Joseph Rowntree Foundation and a financial contribution from the NSPCC. It would not have been possible without the cooperation and generosity of an NSPCC team and their clients, who shared their professional practice and experience. The research was also aided by Susan Taylor and the Advisory Group for the project, who asked many valuable questions and provided critical reading as the work progressed. The Advisory Group comprised Bruce Clark, Mike Fisher, Jenny Gray, Carol-Ann Hooper, Bill Selwyn, Ann Sinclair and Lorna Smith.

The views expressed here are those of the authors and do not necessarily represent the views of any other organisation involved in the research.

# Executive summary

Prior to the research project, the NSPCC team in question had found in a few instances that focusing on domestic violence could have a directly positive effect on their ongoing preventative and recovery work with abused children. The research set out to examine the impact on the team's work of introducing a systematic means of identifying domestic violence and of incorporating the issue in professional practice with children who have been abused.

Generally, the research and focus on domestic violence allowed child abuse cases to be looked at in a wider context, leading to more realistic, holistic and sophisticated practice responses. The number of instances involving domestic violence became more obvious as the research progressed: there was evidence of domestic violence in one third of the child abuse cases prior to the research and this rose to two thirds during the research period. It also became apparent that with regard to this particular sample, in most cases the domestic violence and sexual abuse to the child was carried out by the same perpetrator, who was also the child's father or father figure.

## Summary of main findings

*Identifying domestic violence*

- Before the project, the team would not have asked clients about domestic violence.

- Involvement in the project had 'allowed' domestic violence to be talked about and acknowledged.

- Use of the monitoring form had raised awareness of domestic violence, had given staff permission to ask service users about domestic violence, had given service users permission to disclose domestic violence, and had acted as an 'aide memoire' to ask about domestic violence.

- During the course of the research domestic violence was increasingly being identified and integrated into the team's practice with children.

*Incorporating domestic violence in child protection practice*

- Incorporating domestic violence provided a wider context for understanding children's situations and experiences.

- The use of 'reframing' to incorporate domestic violence had enabled examination of alternative practice options that could enhance work with abused children.

- The project had enabled the team to see children as experiencing both child abuse and domestic violence from the same man.

- The project had led the team to consider domestic violence as a child protection issue.

- Focusing on domestic violence allowed the team to incorporate a wider range of child abuse in their work, in that living with domestic violence was being seen as abusive to children.

- Combining domestic violence and child abuse issues provided more safety-oriented options at times.

- The issue of domestic violence moved from the periphery to the centre of the team's work in child abuse prevention.

- By the end of the project acknowledgement of the interconnectedness of domestic violence and the safety and welfare of children was integrated more fully into practice.

*Work with non-abusive carers/mothers*

- The project led to an increase in work with both child and mother (usually the non-abusive carer).

- A better understanding of domestic violence had allowed challenging of mother-blaming approaches.

- Incorporating knowledge of domestic violence into practice had led to work with mothers and children which the team saw as positive for children.

- The project led to women being seen in a different light, as possibly both abusive and non-abusive carers.

- Positive interagency links had been developed as a result of the project.

*Difficulties*

- Domestic violence raises real issues that can be difficult, including personally for workers.

- Incorporating/focusing on domestic violence can feel overwhelming for workers.

- A greater awareness of domestic violence issues for women and children does not obviously show how to work with men who are violent.

- Introducing a new 'system' of working is time-consuming and requires commitment.

## Conclusion

As the project progressed clear changes were discerned within the team, both in relation to awareness of domestic violence and in relation to professional practice. This involved the change from seeing domestic violence as an issue, but usually as separate from children and child abuse, to seeing it as possibly a central issue for children, and as a part of their abusive experiences. There was a move towards a more integrated, 'holistic' approach where the domestic violence context was taken into account, leading to more effective work with women and children.

The use of both monitoring and reframing to enable the incorporation of domestic violence as an issue in child protection work would also be transferable to other practice settings.

# Part One: Background

# Introduction

The project set out to examine the implications of incorporating domestic violence (that is, primarily, violence against women by their male partners) in the practice of an NSPCC team in their work with children who had been referred to them because of abuse. The team involved in the project carried out mainly recovery work with children who had experienced sexual abuse.

## Background

Increasingly, research and policy have pointed to the importance of considering domestic violence as an issue in child protection and abuse prevention. Not only is the abuse of children, both directly and indirectly, likely to occur in a context of domestic violence, but the practice of childcare professionals may be more positive and effective where domestic violence is taken into account (Farmer and Owen, 1995; Hester and Radford, 1996; Abrahams, 1994; Mullender and Morley, 1994; Hester et al, 1998; DoH, 1997; Stark and Flitcraft, 1988; London Borough of Hackney, 1993; Ball, 1995).

Both child protection research and research focusing more specifically on domestic violence has found that this is a context where there is likely to be risk of significant harm to children. The child protection studies in the UK indicate that domestic violence is often a significant and consistent feature whatever form of abuse a child is deemed to present – whether physical, sexual or emotional abuse. While these studies have not tended to focus on domestic violence, they none the less suggest that in instances of child abuse between a fifth and nearly two thirds of the children with social services or other child protection involvement were also living in circumstances of domestic violence (Cleaver and Freeman, 1995; Gibbons et al, 1995; Maynard, 1985; Brandon and Lewis, 1996; Farmer and Owen, 1995; Farmer and Pollock, 1998; Humphreys, 1997). The more detailed the studies the more likely they were to find that domestic violence was an issue. Enquiry reports concerning child deaths have also highlighted that children may be at risk of significant harm in contexts of domestic violence, but that this link has usually been ignored or seen as peripheral by child protection professionals (James, 1994; Armstrong, 1994; O'Hara, 1994).

Research focusing specifically on domestic violence has consistently revealed that there is a link between domestic violence and physical and/or sexual abuse of children. For instance, Edleson (1995), in an overview of American studies, suggests that in 32% to 53% of all families where women are being physically beaten by their partners, the children are also the victims of direct abuse by the same perpetrator. Studies from the UK provide similar figures (see Hanmer, 1989; Abrahams, 1994; Hester and Radford, 1996; and see Hester et al, 1998, ch 2 for overview). The research has also indicated that the majority of children living in circumstances of domestic violence witness the violence and abusive behaviour to their mothers (Dobash and Dobash, 1984; Andrews and Brown, 1988; Abrahams, 1994). Witnessing violence to their mothers, and/or living in the context of violence, can have a detrimental impact on children, and may be seen as emotional abuse or psychological maltreatment (Saunders et al, 1995; Abrahams, 1994; Brandon and Lewis, 1996; Jaffe et al, 1990; Christensen, 1990; Carroll, 1994; and see Kolbo et al, 1996).

Research has generally indicated that:

- the domestic violence perpetrator may also be directly – physically and or sexually – abusing the child(ren) living in the household;

- witnessing/living with violence to their mothers may have an abusive impact on the children concerned;

- the perpetrators may abuse the child as a part of their violence against their (usually) female partners (Hester et al, 1998).

In relation to child protection there has often been an expectation, by social services professionals in particular, that it is the role of mothers to protect their children from violent partners, either by leaving the relationship or by controlling the man's violent behaviour (Humphreys, 1997). At the same time the violence and abuse women have experienced from male partners has tended to be ignored. It is thus mothers who have usually been constructed as the problem rather than the violent and abusive men (O'Hagan and Dillenburger, 1995; Farmer and Owen, 1995; Stark and Flitcraft, 1988). Yet, incorporating knowledge and understanding of domestic violence might be a potentially positive approach in child protection cases (Jaffe et al, 1990; Kelly, 1994; Mullender and Morley, 1994). Moreover, working to ensure the safety of mothers can be protective of children. This has been recognised in recent Labour government policy. As the Department of Health (DoH) Circular on Part IV of the Family Law Act (1997) suggests,

> Where domestic violence may be an important element in the family, the safety of (usually) the mother is also in the child's welfare. (p 12)

## The research project

We set out to examine how professionals working with children who have been abused might incorporate the issue of domestic violence and the impact on their work of so doing. It was decided to carry out the research with an NSPCC team as the focus. The team's activities gave the researchers access to a range of work with abused children, mainly recovery, and to a lesser extent investigative. The emphasis by the team on recovery work provided the researchers with useful detail and insight into the overall processes and potential problems involved in incorporating the issue of domestic violence into work with abused children. While the nature of the team's work made it somewhat different to, for example, many social services teams, it was felt that the findings would none the less be of relevance to a variety of agencies.

Prior to the development of the research project, the NSPCC team in question had found to a limited extent that focusing on domestic violence could have a directly positive effect on their ongoing preventative and recovery work with children. By incorporating the issue of domestic violence, they had been able to change a number of situations where there would have been a need for child protection in the longer term, to situations where abuse was prevented. In one example, through a refocusing on domestic violence by a number of agencies involved, a mother who was previously perceived as obstructive to agency intervention, was provided with support for herself and for prevention of abuse to her children.

In its 1995 'Cry for Children' campaign, the NSPCC nationally had expressed the importance of addressing directly the issue of domestic violence in relation to work with children. However, neither they, nor other similar agencies, had any systematic means of identifying domestic violence, or of incorporating the issue in practice. It became apparent that the detailed research on women's experiences and professional practice with regard to domestic violence, which we had previously carried out (Hester and Radford, 1996; Hester et al, 1997), would provide a useful framework and basis for developing a means of allowing identification and disclosure of domestic violence in relation to childcare practice. In particular, the development of a monitoring scheme for domestic violence was thought to be useful. This could introduce domestic violence as an issue into the team's work in a systematic way, could help to increase awareness in the team of what domestic violence entails, and could enable disclosure of domestic violence by children and/or their carers or referrers.

In addition, we wanted to chart the impact of the introduction of domestic violence as an issue in the team's work in order to answer the following questions:

- Was it, in terms of the team, desirable or even possible to make such changes?

- Might there be positive lessons to be learnt concerning practice?

- Would incorporation of domestic violence allow the development of effective and safety oriented work in relation to children?

- Had the approach led to work with both mothers and their children where domestic violence had been identified?

Finally, we wanted to examine the implications of incorporating domestic violence for interagency work in relation to children. Interagency working has been identified in policy as an important area for development (Home Office, 1991). Previously, the NSPCC team in question had found, in a small number of cases, that focusing on domestic violence could create possibilities for the establishment of positive interagency links. Such links can often be problematic, however, as agencies have different remits and different approaches (see Roaf and Lloyd, 1995; Hague et al, 1996). Moreover, interagency work concerning children who have been abused tends to be separate from that on domestic violence (Atkinson, 1996; Hester et al, 1998). Therefore, we wanted to examine whether a greater emphasis on domestic violence would have an impact on the team's interagency links and approach to interagency working.

Overall, the project set out with the following aims:

- to develop a monitoring scheme for identifying domestic violence and enabling disclosure of such violence in relation to both children and adults who contact the NSPCC;

- to evaluate the impact on the practice of introducing domestic violence as an issue into the team's work with children;

- to identify the longer-term implications of a domestic violence monitoring scheme for the work of the NSPCC and other agencies working with children, including establishment of interagency links.

## Definition of domestic violence

From the outset, the researchers and the team discussed and decided on a definition of 'domestic violence' to use in the project. An inclusive definition was adopted, reflecting the experiences described by women (predominantly) in such situations (Dobash and Dobash, 1980; Kelly, 1988; Hester and Radford, 1996). Included in the definition were any controlling or undermining behaviours which were seen to result in one adult exerting 'power and control over' another in the context of an intimate relationship (whether this be marriage, living together or apart, etc). Domestic violence was deemed to include many forms of behaviour and to be described through a wide range of terms. Cases involving domestic violence were thus seen to include one or more of the following behaviours:

- physical violence (eg, assaulting, hitting, punching);

- sexual abuse (eg, rape, buggery);

- emotional abuse (eg, withholding love);

- psychological abuse (eg, threat to injure woman and/or child);

- threats to kill (eg, verbal and non-verbal);

- verbal abuse (eg, 'fat slag', 'stupid');

- financial control (eg, withholding money).

The definition of domestic violence was also revisited and discussed with the NSPCC team as the research progressed. It became clear that at different times team members would apply variations of the originally agreed definition. One recurring issue concerned whether or not domestic violence included violence and abuse of children, rather than exclusively violence and abuse of adults in (or previously in) an intimate relationship. There was also ongoing discussion of whether violence from teenagers to their mothers, for instance, constituted 'domestic violence'. For the purposes of the research it was agreed that the working definition of 'domestic violence' should be seen as violence and abuse experienced by adults, and 'child abuse' as relating to children. However, one member of the team tended to apply a wider definition where abuse of children was also incorporated in 'domestic violence' in situations where children were deemed to have been directly affected by living in circumstances of domestic violence, and this was taken into account in the analysis.

## Methodology

The project was carried out in close cooperation between the researchers and the NSPCC team, using a 'reflective practitioner' approach (Everitt et al, 1992; Shakespeare et al, 1993). The project began at the beginning of August 1996 and was completed in March 1998.

In order to introduce the issue of domestic violence into the work of the team, two main approaches were adopted:

- use of team meetings to discuss definitions of domestic violence and to examine the incorporation of domestic violence through 'reframing' of past and current cases;

- the development of a simple monitoring scheme for domestic violence to be applied across the team's work.

The monitoring scheme was piloted during December 1996 and January 1997.

In order to ascertain and chart any changes concerning the practice of the team with regard to domestic violence and child abuse prevention, a multi-method approach was adopted. This included:

- interviews with individual members of the team

- analysis of case files

- analysis of monitoring forms

- meetings with the team.

This multi-method approach enabled some triangulation of data and provided a means of ensuring reliability and validity of the data. In addition, some observation of practice was carried out to help the researchers understand the practice of the team in greater depth. It was also considered important to determine the impact on service users of being asked about

domestic violence. To this end, the team's existing service user evaluation form (for both adults and children) was modified to include a simple question about their reactions to being asked about domestic violence.

Individual interviews with team members took place at three stages during the process of the research, to coincide with:

- the start of the project;

- the end of the pilot monitoring period; and

- the end of the main fieldwork period (end of case file period B – see below).

Case files were examined in relation to three separate periods (case file periods A, B and C), and files were only looked at where the cases had been closed (that is, there was no longer any active involvement by the team). The case file periods were as follows:

- **case file period A** – the 12 months before the onset of the research project (between 1 August 1995 and 31 July 1996);

- **case file period B** – the first 12 months of the project (between 1 August 1996 and 31 July 1997);

- **case file period C** – the six-month period following on from period B (between 1 August 1997 and 31 January 1998).

(See Figure 1 for further details regarding the chronology of the project.)

Throughout this report, case file periods A and B are referred to together as 'the main case file research period', as they involved systematic and detailed analysis of all case files. In case file period C, we examined only those cases identified by the team as involving domestic violence and a general analysis of the file data was not carried out.

A monitoring form was piloted during December 1996 and January 1997 and monitoring then continued until the end of the project. Forms relating to the pilot monitoring period and until the end of January 1998 were analysed.

See Appendix A for further details regarding the methodology.

Figure 1: Chronology of the project

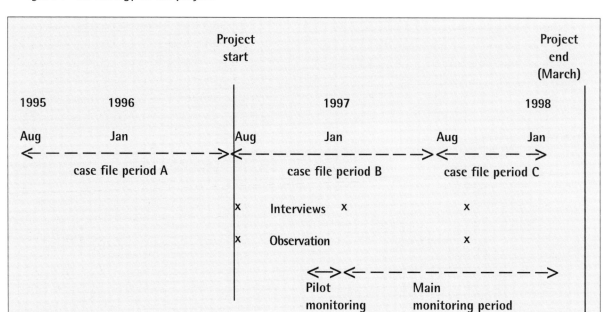

## The work of the NSPCC team

### Staffing and practice approaches

The team involved in the project were typical of the smaller NSPCC services. During the period of the research the number of staff fluctuated, from a maximum of two-and-a-half full-time (equivalent) child protection officers, a half-time therapist, one full-time team manager and two full-time administrative staff, to one-and-a-half full-time (equivalent) child protection officers, a half-time therapist, a half-time team manager and one-and-a-half administrative staff. In addition there were four students on placement for various parts of the project. All members of staff were crucial to the implementation of the research project (see Appendix B, Table 1 for staffing details during the research period).

In the team's recovery work a variety of practice approaches was drawn upon, such as play therapy, drama therapy, art therapy and family therapy, with an emphasis on integration and on the process being client-led. The main focus of all the work undertaken was the abuse of the child, and this included focusing on a range of areas, such as self-esteem work, keeping safe work, looking at 'muddles', or exploring anxieties/feelings/difficulties through play and art.

The team were also interested in the application of what they termed a 'systemic' approach because they saw that as allowing them to examine the context for the child who had been abused, including the individual(s) involved and the significant relationships for the child. They did not use the 'classic' family therapy approach because of its omission of notions of power and gender, which they saw as resulting in a lack of a dynamic understanding of the family. Instead, they were wanting to enable the child to be safe through incorporating and understanding the child's contexts and relationships, and by working in conjunction with the caring adults as well as directly with the child.

In a sense this mirrored the more general change in policy which has taken place regarding child protection. This has placed emphasis on a broader 'needs' based approach, involving partnership with parents and agencies, rather than focusing on specific incidents of abuse (Home Office, 1991; 1995). Where the team was concerned, this change in approach had enabled them, and the service users, to decide when to see children individually, when to see children and their parent(s) (or other carers/adults), or perhaps to only see the parent. Previously they had always tended to see the child alone.

## Work carried out

During the main period of the research (across case file periods A and B), the overall number of referrals to the team was 267, 131 in period A and 136 in period B. Of these, 111 cases were accepted for service by the team, 59 in case file period A and 52 in period B. The rest were either referred out to other agencies (53 in A and 44 in B), in particular social services, or involved no further action (19 in A and 40 in B) (see Appendix B, Table 2 for details).

The focus of the team's work was on children who have experienced abuse, of which the major concern tended to be sexual abuse. In the main case file periods, towards half of the requests for service involved sexual abuse as the key focus of concern. This rose to three quarters of the cases accepted for service. About a fifth of the requests involved cases of physical abuse, but less than 15% of these were accepted for service. No cases involving neglect were accepted for service (see Appendix B, Table 4).

Most requests concerned recovery work for children who had been abused, and there were a small number of requests for specialist investigations or assessments of risk. The majority of these were accepted for service (see Appendix B, Table 3). In both case file periods A and B counselling and treatment/recovery constituted more than three quarters of the cases accepted for service, together increasing from 78% in period A to 84.6% in period B. Assessment and investigation comprised 13.6% of accepted work in period A, decreasing to 1.9% of accepted work in period B (due largely to decrease in available staff).

Service users themselves contacted the NSPCC to request support, or other agencies made the initial referral – such as social services, doctors or schools. The requests for service were most likely to come from parents and other carers, social services, other agencies (such as education or health) and members of the public. There were a few requests from children, who were most likely to contact the NSPCC regarding physical abuse (see Appendix B, Tables 5 and 6).

## Profile of service users – children

The total number of children who were considered as subjects of the service request was 177 in case file period A and 200 in period B. Children were classed as subjects of the service request on the basis of either having been directly abused or indirectly affected by abuse taking place within the family. The majority of these children (where known) were girls – information was available for 160 of the children in case file period A and 188 in period B (see Appendix B, Table 7). Children between the ages of 5 and 14 predominated in both groups. In many cases the age of the child presenting for service and the age of the child at the time of the abuse were different, because the NSPCC's recovery work would only occur once investigations and legal processes had been completed. There were also some older children who needed to work on the sexual abuse they had experienced when they were younger, and which was re-emerging as an issue because of their own sexual and emotional development.

Only limited information regarding the race and ethnicity was available for the children in the accepted for service files. Race/ethnicity was specified for 26 of the 64 children (or 40.6%) in the sample accepted for service, and for 23 of the 72 children (or 31.9%) in the sample accepted for service in period B. There was no specific monitoring by the team with regard to disability and information about this was gleaned from different parts of the files. Disability was mentioned in relation to a total of 17 children across case file periods A and B.

## Profile of service users – adults

The range of adults identified as subjects of the request for service included mothers, fathers, partners, step-parents, foster/adoptive parents and other carers. Mothers and their children predominated as services users, while fathers were less frequently involved (see Appendix B, Table 8). Few specific details were given about the race/ethnicity of the adults who were subjects of the request for service. Similarly, the information concerning disability was sparse and featured as an issue for only two of the mothers in period B.

# Part Two: Introducing domestic violence into practice

Prior to the project, there was no mechanism by which team members would necessarily know whether or not domestic violence was a relevant issue for the service users they were seeing. Any such information was likely to be provided incidentally. As one team member pointed out "We would only know if somebody told us", and they would not usually ask clients directly about any experience of domestic violence. None the less, incidents were mentioned in the case files prior to the project.

As one means of introducing the issue of domestic violence into the team's work with children, a monitoring scheme was devised. The implementation of the resultant monitoring forms, coupled with the interviews and analysis of case files provided ways of charting change in practice. Chapter 2 examines the implementation of the monitoring scheme.

The other approach was by 'reframing' of cases to examine what might have happened in practice if domestic violence had been identified as a part of the focus in the work carried out. Chapter 3 outlines the use of reframing.

# 2

# The introduction and application of domestic violence monitoring

As outlined in Chapter 1 and in Appendix A, a simple monitoring form was devised for use in all the work carried out by the NSPCC team. This was piloted to allow for comments and additions before the main monitoring period began in January 1997.

## The pilot period

The pilot monitoring forms were introduced for a six-week period during December 1996 and January 1997. The format and content of the form was agreed following discussions with the NSPCC team. The monitoring of domestic violence (through 'screening') had already been developed for use in mediation, primarily outside the UK (Girdner, 1989; Astor, 1991; 1994; Magana and Taylor, 1993). While this had been useful within mediation, the screening processes employed were not entirely relevant to agencies such as the NSPCC who were working to counter the abuse of children. This was mainly because the client groups and the reasons for contacting or being referred to an agency, tended to be different. However, the experience gained from the previous 'Domestic Violence and Child Contact' research project (Hester and Radford, 1996) and the existing screening procedures in mediation, provided a basis for the scheme adopted in this project. Here, the scheme was specifically developed to incorporate means of identifying domestic violence, creation of a context for disclosure of domestic violence by children and/or adults, and awareness-building for practitioners.

One of the problems with introducing a monitoring scheme was to ensure that it would fit with the ways in which the team worked. As most of the work of the team concerned recovery and counselling and the use of client-led approaches, there was often an emphasis on 'listening' to clients rather than on any systematic asking of questions. Initially, we had thought that a monitoring form, with a set of questions about possible experiences related to domestic violence, could be used in conjunction with current intake and referral procedures. However, after discussion with the team and some observation of team practice, it was decided that a multi-stage monitoring approach should be adopted so that disclosure of domestic violence might occur at any stage in the practice process, and from clients or referrers. Thus, the scheme adopted involved a form to be completed at the referral stage of every case, and after every subsequent contact with service users.

This consisted of a set of questions related to domestic violence – violence and abuse in the adult's relationship – and a set of questions regarding any impact on the child resulting from the domestic violence. There was a question concerning how the worker obtained any knowledge about the domestic violence, that is from the adult client, child client or referrer (see Appendix C for layout of monitoring form). It was also decided to introduce a monitoring form for the workers to use in their supervision sessions in order to record any instances where the workers suspected domestic violence was an issue, but where this had not been mentioned directly by the service users.

## Monitoring forms for clients

Discussions with the team following the pilot monitoring period revealed that pilot forms had not been completed in *every* case, partly because it was at times too difficult or inappropriate to ask. This was especially so at the point of referral of a case which was not going to be accepted for service, or when the referral concerned abuse outside the family. This difficulty also applied with existing cases, where forms were not necessarily completed after every point of contact, particularly if no new information had emerged concerning domestic violence. It was felt by staff that their practice approach with certain clients could also make it difficult to ask the set of questions from the form. This led to the decision to add an 'inappropriate to ask/not asked' box, so that in theory *every* case in the main monitoring period would include at least one form.

In reality, however, forms were not completed in every case in this way. Throughout the project, some difficulties remained with establishing and maintaining this monitoring system, and there was continued hesitation about using the monitoring form in all cases and at all points of contact. In interviews, some team members talked about the difficulties of incorporating questions about domestic violence into their practice, and how it might be inappropriate or unsafe if the male partner was present:

> "Sometimes when I have a family in and there's been no reference to domestic violence at all within the referral, I find it difficult to talk about.... Where I've been working though with just mothers, or mothers and children, or just children, or families where domestic violence has been part of the referral, it's been a lot easier.... I suppose it's because the man is there – that's what makes it difficult."

This was found to be particularly problematic in relation to duty calls, perhaps involving only one contact, as opposed to the more long-term and in-depth accepted for work cases. This was often compounded by pressures of work:

> "... my bet is that ... a higher proportion of substantive [accepted] ones would be filled out, but it's the ones where you're dashing about, you're in-between sessions, or whatever it might be, you take a duty call, and, you know, I know for a fact I haven't filled out some of those...."

In some of these duty calls, when people were often in crisis, it could also appear inappropriate to ask about domestic violence, especially when the relevance of this might not be apparent to the caller. As one team member explained:

> "... it could be stressful if you don't actually want to approach that subject at that time – actually ringing up because you've got the courage to ring up and say, 'I've been sexually abused – or the child has'. And then suddenly you're pushed into this area, also of great need, that they may not necessarily put together as being connected terrifically, so that could be difficult...."

Clearly, the use of the monitoring form took a long time to be adopted systematically in the team's work. Another reason given was that the monitoring forms were separate from the other main form used to record referrals and could, therefore, quite easily be forgotten. Several members of the team suggested that domestic violence monitoring should somehow be integrated into the main referral form:

> "I've found it's been a very useful thing to do and though we'll presumably stop using the forms eventually, I hope that it'll be sort of put in somewhere on the forms we actually use. I guess that's what everyone hopes."

> "I'd really like to see it [domestic violence] on our form 18s [referral forms], actually as a category."

However, despite these difficulties, interviews with team members indicated that the existence of the forms was having an impact on the general awareness of domestic violence, and that they were seen as enabling a focus on issues of relevance to practice:

> "The very existence of the forms I think has meant that we have concentrated more on whether domestic violence is an issue."

> "[talking about a particular instance] ... there you are, an example of violence to the adults and nobody really worries too much about it, even though it might well affect the children if they were to see it. And I was thinking, you know, when

doing it, when I remember to do the forms, that it was a pretty good idea because it focuses things."

And as another team member pointed out, the form and the research had enabled her to ask in cases where she had previously suspected domestic violence:

"... there's two cases I've got that I was working with before you came, and one of them I did suspect domestic violence and I have now asked because the monitoring form has enabled me to ask."

## Supervision forms

A slightly different form was developed for use in supervision, partly to enable staff to voice concerns about domestic violence where this had not been brought up by clients themselves. The total number (including both pilot and main monitoring period) of completed supervision forms for individual cases (that is, counting one form per case) was 13.

During the pilot stage there were staff supervision sessions with regard to 11 cases. Staff identified domestic violence as a concern in four of these, and children were directly affected in all of them. The domestic violence consisted of physical violence in all four cases. In addition, one situation was also seen to involve psychological and verbal abuse, and another sexual, psychological, verbal and financial abuse.

There were only two additional forms used during supervision after the pilot phase. During the pilot, the use of the supervision monitoring forms had been seen as useful when they were, in effect, used as a further 'check' that the system was being implemented. Later on, this became unnecessary and they tended not to be used.

## Impact of monitoring

Several issues emerged for the team in relation to domestic violence monitoring. Among these was the question of how to ask about domestic violence without diverting the focus from the main presenting issue, as described by a worker in relation to one particular situation:

"I think the main feeling was that it [asking about domestic violence] would have taken things down the wrong track. It would have gone away from the main issue that was being presented at that time."

This issue of maintaining a balanced focus on child abuse could be of particular concern when domestic violence was more difficult to establish. This could lead to some anxieties about keeping the centrality of child abuse at the perceived expense of discovering domestic violence issues:

"... sometimes where it's [domestic violence] not quite as obvious as that where somebody isn't saying it so explicitly, that there are a lot of things to remember and, with the focus being child abuse and also what happens if I don't get the child abuse bits right, and concerns over that, that maybe at times it [domestic violence monitoring] has taken second place...."

A different anxiety was expressed by another worker in that she experienced a sense of failure with one family when she did not manage to ask about domestic violence:

"... this one particular family when I just couldn't get my mind round to asking them. I sort of made a space several times during the interview but I just couldn't do it because they had so many problems.... I just couldn't get through that lot to kind of, 'Oh well, and is there any domestic violence as well'... So I felt I'd failed."

There were also concerns about the appropriateness of using the monitoring forms with children to raise domestic violence issues. This did not necessarily 'fit' very easily with the client-led emphasis of the team and could feel overly intrusive, especially as domestic violence was not usually the presenting issue for the child. One worker explained her preference for using the monitoring form with the adults, and then to explore any issues raised directly or indirectly by the child in the subsequent therapeutic sessions:

"... you can ask it [domestic violence] when you have them [the family] in initial assessment or interview with somebody. If you're just working with the child, sometimes it feels like prying, unless it comes up. So I try and ask it, if at all possible, when I'm showing them round or when I'm having an initial 'What help do you think you need from us?' with the parent rather than with the child because I think if you're just working with the child on sexual abuse, say, it's not always easy to bring domestic violence.... If they started playing violent activities in a family context with the dolls house or something, then I would. So I think sometimes I've asked things like 'Who sorts out arguments in your house?' – that kind of way round. But it's easier to do it with the parents...."

Overall, despite these concerns, workers felt that the experience of using the monitoring forms had been positive, and the benefits included:

- giving service users permission to disclose domestic violence;

- giving permission to ask service users about domestic violence;

- acting as an 'aide memoire' to ask about domestic violence.

All the team pointed to the need for domestic violence monitoring to become a more integrated part of their referral system. Even if the use of the form did not continue, or become integrated in this way, the project would have had a lasting impact on practice, as one member of the team explained:

"... even if it isn't, it'll be much more. It'll be a prominent thought in my mind now when I actually have referrals or when I talk to people, and though it was always an issue, I think it will be more like seeking the information rather than waiting for it to come out in a session or not at all even, because they don't actually always come to sessions, so sometimes you might not have the opportunity to meet with them."

# 3

# Reframing to take domestic violence into account

In order to explore the use of a 'domestic violence focused' framework in the team's work, some of the team meetings were used to re-examine and reframe certain cases. Previously closed cases were selected where the research examination of the files had identified domestic violence but where this had not been made apparent or explicit by the NSPCC team, or where its existence remained as a possibility in the background.

This reframing exercise involved the exploration of the effect that taking domestic violence into account might have had on each individual case. In this way, domestic violence was used as one of the 'lenses' through which to look at the practice which was carried out. This reframing proved a very useful mechanism for the integration of work around both child abuse and domestic violence. As one team member explained, these re-examinations of cases were helpful in considering alternative practice possibilities and, in particular, clarified for her how the 'domestic violence lens' could enhance her work with children:

"... the thing that brought it home to me was ... when we looked at some cases, we traced the domestic violence, we traced the problems back ... and it sort of really brought it home to me that there we all were, all the different agencies, running round in circles basically trying to help families, not actually considering the issue of the domestic violence and how problems that had either arisen from that or been exacerbated by that, and that in fact we probably had to go back and deal with that domestic violence issue to make any headway at

all and to get people in a stable sort of settled environment, to be able to benefit from some therapy and get their lives back on course."

These discussions also led to a reframing of some of the other cases which had been or were currently being worked with by the team, where the presenting problem was a child's disruptive behaviour. Looking at domestic violence issues in some of these cases provided a much wider context for understanding that behaviour, and thus more effective intervention where the child was not pathologised:

"I also feel that the children themselves, either with their parent or independently, individually, need space to work through their experience of domestic violence and see it's different. And people don't always listen to children or realise how affected they are even when the mother is much stronger. And sometimes, of course, when a mother is stronger, that's when a child starts to exhibit various behaviours because they're now able to show how they felt about it."

This was exactly what happened in another instance:

"She was having difficulties with her little girl's behaviour ... when the little girl got angry, she's very angry because her father wouldn't let her have any of her belongings ever. He's still got all her toys – everything. And her mum kept saying things like, but I'm sure you're too big for them. 'But they're mine and I want them.' And she started kicking and biting and scratching her mum again. And I said, 'Well maybe she sees you as the strong person now and forgets what it was like – so she doesn't see why you can't go and get them, so just talk to her about what it was like…. So just explore that anger with her and tell her, you know, mummy is angry too, mummy can't have any of her things.' But this is what the judge said about it. So that's what she did the next time she got angry and, yes, it worked, and the little girl kind of had a long conversation with her mother about it."

Discussing these cases in this way thus highlighted for the team how domestic violence had remained very much a peripheral concern, where issues for the child had not been explored or understood. It emphasised the need to put child protection concerns into the domestic violence framework, and to look at the impact of domestic violence on the child in a much broader context.

In addition to this, looking at cases through the domestic violence 'lens' led to the reframing of some cases as involving domestic violence as well as child abuse. For instance, in one particular case the team had investigated an allegation that the key worker of a 16-year-old girl in residential care was involved with her in a sexual relationship. This was an allegation made by the girl herself, but was subsequently retracted. The man involved was consequently suspended for abusing his position of authority. The team had identified the case as involving child sexual abuse, even though the young woman concerned considered herself in some ways to be in a relationship with this man:

> "[we] had undertaken an investigation and, whilst we had, without naming as domestic violence, attended to some of the domestic violence issues around the young woman being with – having a sexual relationship with a man who abused his power, so we did address some of those issues as though we were naming it as domestic violence, but we very clearly gave it very much a child abuse emphasis."

As the investigation by the team progressed, they learnt more details about the young

woman's relationship with this man, including instances where he had put his hands around her throat in a very threatening way. On at least two occasions she reported that when he was displeased with her "he was rough and angry … he pushed her, but did not hit her". In another instance, "he frightened her by shaking her violently". There were also suggestions by her that he was being sexually coercive in that she described how "he wouldn't leave her alone".

Therefore, this case could, at the same time as involving child abuse, also be looked at as an instance of domestic violence, although it was not labelled as such by the team at the time. Reframing in this way did not alter the impropriety or nature of the man's behaviour. It did, however, provide an *additional* way in which the team could have carried out recovery work with the young woman, and would have allowed them to work in a child/person-centred way that incorporated her own apparent perspective. Incorporating domestic violence into the picture would also have allowed information regarding refuges and other support for women experiencing domestic violence to be imparted in relation to safety planning with the young woman. In retrospect, this was recognised by the team members who had carried out the original investigation work with this young woman:

> "… if we kind of named it better to ourselves, we might have been able to just name it that bit better to her; and I think we set out by naming it child abuse without the domestic violence – this is the key thing … here was somebody of 15 [at the time the sexual relationship began] who was desperate to be a young woman as well as a child, so if we'd been able to say, well, actually you're being abused as a woman, I think it would have helped us to get into a kind of different partnership with her maybe … because … we might have been able to say, 'Hey, would you like to go and talk to so-and-so because she might have thought, well, I wouldn't mind going to talk to somebody, another woman, a refuge, or a domestic violence family advice line' – because they don't have to take this child abuse approach."

This was identified as a problematic issue across the agency as a whole where 15-year-olds are concerned and where the focus of intervention is on the child, rather than on the possibly abusive dynamics of their relationships:

"What I notice with some sort of disappointment is that despite those debates, we're still doing that; we're still very much defending taking very much a child abuse framework without the attendant domestic violence framework – you know, when we've got a 15-year-old girl or something like that – and my problem with that is that I think that's across the agency as well."

Thus, the re-examination and reframing of previous cases in order to incorporate domestic violence as a possible key feature in the lives of the children concerned provided a much wider view and context for understanding their presenting behaviour. This was also seen by the team to result in more effective work with both children and parents/carers.

# Part Three: The results

An important aim of the project was to ascertain whether, and if so how, the introduction of domestic violence as an issue in the NSPCC team's work impacted on their practice. As outlined in Chapters 2 and 3, domestic violence as an issue of relevance to work with children had been introduced to the team via a number of routes, principally through discussions in team meetings, including use of reframing, and by the development and application of a monitoring scheme. Charting change is difficult and we decided to reflect the possible complexities by employing a number of different ways in which to highlight and 'measure' possible changes in practice. Three ways in particular were used:

- analysis of the language used in case files in order to identify instances involving domestic violence and how the issue of domestic violence might be incorporated into practice;

- analysis of monitoring forms;

- analysis of individual and team interviews.

This part of the report documents these analyses and any resultant changes observed with regard to the team's practice. The next four chapters detail issues of language, the results from the monitoring forms and the case files, an exploration of findings in relation to domestic violence and children and the impact of these on practice. Information from the interviews is integrated throughout these chapters as relevant.

# 4

# Identification of domestic violence

Case files exist for every request for service which is made of the NSPCC (see Appendix A). These may contain anything from the nature of the request to detailed notes of initial sessions, contacts with other agencies and supervision of the staff involved. We were given access to files once they had been 'closed', that is, where there was no longer any active involvement from the NSPCC team. Any 'open' files, where work of some kind was still in progress, were excluded to ensure that the research did not become invasive for either the service users or the workers.

The case files were examined in relation to the three separate 'case file periods' A, B and C (see Chapter 1 for overall chronology):

**case file period A:** all the files closed in the 12 months before the onset of the research project (between 1 August 1995 and 31 July 1996).

**case file period B:** all files closed during the first 12 months of the research project (between 1 August 1996 and 31 July 1997).

**case file period C:** files closed during the next six months, which was also the latter end of the project (between 1 August 1997 and 31 January 1998). In this period only the files where cases were accepted for service *and* identified by the team as involving domestic violence were examined.

While these three sets of files formed a continuum in terms of the NSPCC team's work and cannot therefore be seen as entirely separate and finite (especially as some cases became 'open' and 'closed' at different points during the research), the division into A, B and C was

nevertheless a useful means of charting impact on practice.

As indicated, the sets of files were not all examined in the same way. All the closed files in periods A and B were analysed in detail by the researchers and thus provided comparable data. However, time constraints prevented a similarly detailed analysis of the files in case file period C. These were only examined if the NSPCC team had already identified the existence of domestic violence. While not directly comparable to the data in case file periods A and B, the more limited data from case file period C was none the less important to take into consideration, as the domestic violence monitoring system had become more fully established during these final months of the project. According to the NSPCC team, changes in practice in relation to domestic violence were becoming more apparent at the period C stage.

After initial analysis of a small number of files for piloting purposes it was decided to focus on two types of data from the files in periods A and B:

- *Words or narrative* indicative of the existence of domestic violence were extracted from the case files for separate analysis. This was carried out in order to identify instances of domestic violence. Information about where such information had originated was recorded (for example, from the abused, from the abuser, from the child, from the referrer), as was the location in the file. This provided a means of determining who appeared to be defining a behaviour as domestic violence, and to examine if there were any differences or similarities if it was defined as domestic violence by the abused, by the NSPCC team or by the researchers.

- *Coding of parameters* in the case files was carried out. This concerned the nature of the presenting abuse, any indication of domestic violence, the individuals involved and the work carried out by the NSPCC. Anonymity was ensured. The coded data was entered on to an SPSS database for quantitative analysis.

In addition to this, more limited data from the files in case file period C were also extracted, with a focus on words or narrative used to indicate domestic violence.

## Words or narrative indicative of domestic violence

It was anticipated that the term 'domestic violence' would not necessarily be used in the files, even when it was present (see Kelly and Radford, 1996; Hester et al, 1998). Because of this, a screening mechanism was devised whereby cases involving domestic violence could be detected through the use of particular terms and language. In discussions with the team, an inclusive definition of domestic violence had been agreed which included actual physical violence as well as a range of other controlling and abusive behaviours (see Chapter 1). An important aspect of this definition was the need to focus on the *impact* of the behaviour on each individual rather than assuming that there was some hierarchy of forms of abusive behaviour, which necessarily placed physical abuse as the most 'serious' form of domestic violence. In reality there is much overlap between different domestic violence behaviours, all of which serve to create a situation where one person is able to exert power and control over another. In particular, there appears to be much overlap between the undermining and controlling behaviours which an abuser may use and the directly aggressive or violent behaviours (see Hester and Radford, 1996; Hester et al, 1998).

By applying such a definition of domestic violence in the analysis of the case files in periods A and B, eight sets of terms became apparent, covering behaviour and impact as follows:

- mention of woman staying in a refuge – either currently or in the past;

- mention of 'domestic violence' or injunctions;

- controlling behaviour – this included any behaviour which questioned the abused's right to autonomy and/or where the man (usually) tried to impose his authority;

- undermining behaviour – this included behaviour which aimed to belittle the abused, often in the presence of others;

- direct violence – this included any indication of direct physical or sexual violence, which might also result in some injury being caused;

- violent/aggressive behaviour – this was assumed to indicate mainly physical violence;

- impact on the child;

- impact on the woman/survivor.

Each of these eight categories was exemplified by sets of words or phrases within the files (see Table 1). It is important to recognise that, while we have extracted them here for illustrative purposes, these words and phrases were situated, and understood, within the wider context of the file records.

Looking at the language used in the case files to describe domestic violence and separating the possible behaviours involved in this way allowed a content analysis to be carried out to ascertain whether, and to what extent:

- domestic violence was identified in the files;

- domestic violence was focused on as a practice issue.

It was important in the analysis to place the words and narrative in the wider context of the case, and in this sense we used more of a 'qualitative' approach to content analysis (May, 1997).

## Who identified domestic violence as an issue

An evaluation was made as to whether domestic violence was identified as an issue by the researchers or by the NSPCC team. Across both case file periods A and B, it was clear that there

Table 1: Words or narrative indicating domestic violence in the case files from periods A and B

| Women in refuge | Domestic violence | Controlling | Undermining | Direct violence | Violence/aggression | Impact on child | Impact on woman |
|---|---|---|---|---|---|---|---|
| refuge | domestic violence | manipulate | criticism | hit | assault | hits mum | fear |
| | injunction | harass | insulting comments | beat up | physical abuse | anxious | dependent |
| | 'DV' | oppress | verbal abuse | punched on the head | aggressive | negative to father | frightened of being hit |
| | | dominate | name calling | rape | intimidate | aggression | had counselling |
| | | imposing | 'fat and ugly' | strangle | violent | witnessing attacks | no social life |
| | | powerful | denigrate | shove | rows | dislikes stepfather | no freedom |
| | | threats to leave | 'mad' | throws ashtray | fights | stays in room | wary of his reactions |
| | | not let her use the car | hurtful verbally | bruises | arguments | frightened | affected ability to be an effective parent |
| | | not liking what she wears, where she goes, who her friends are | tarting around | black eye | nasty | unlikely to voice thoughts | lives in constant fear |
| | | intensely jealous | said offensive things | knocked to the ground unconscious | angry | shout or hit to protect mum | powerless |
| | | phoning day and night | gets the better of her in arguments | stabbed in the head | threats | withhold information to protect | leaves in tears |
| | | obsessive towards her | made her look very small | sexually abusive | threats to kill | hysterical | totally under his control |
| | | chose her friends | | split her head open | altercation | scared of play fights | placid and down-trodden |

| Women in refuge | Domestic violence | Controlling | Undermining | Direct violence | Violence/aggression | Impact on child | Impact on woman |
|---|---|---|---|---|---|---|---|
| | | took over life | | broken bones | abusive | going to be beaten up | confused |
| | | arguments about money | | held a knife to throat | fracas | do not want contact | |
| | | stopped her doing a course | | violently shaken | has an awful temper | not happy | |
| | | watches all movement | | use of a knife | throwing/ smashing things | disturbed by incident | |
| | | controls all the money | | | | wishes ignored | |
| | | very possessive | | | | attachment problems | |
| | | no money given | | | | violence to siblings | |
| | | man intercepts her post | | | | shut in room during beating | |
| | | applying for residence of the children | | | | sleeps with a baseball bat | |
| | | | | | | nightmares | |
| | | | | | | fear of being killed | |
| | | | | | | abusive to peers | |
| | | | | | | acted out with knives | |
| | | | | | | withdrawn and upset during | |
| | | | | | | 'rough and tumble' | |
| | | | | | | threats to run away | |
| | | | | | | angry and blame mum | |
| | | | | | | wants to stab/ kill father | |

were cases where similar words and phrases might be used by the NSPCC team to describe domestic violence. These included specific use of the term 'domestic violence', and/or mention of physical acts of violence (such as being hit, being beaten, etc), and/or mention of the woman being/having been in a refuge. Yet, there were differences in the relevance attached to this information. This was also apparent from the more limited analysis of case files in period C.

Overall, it became clear that, over time, 'domestic violence' (however described) moved from a descriptive 'peripheral' location (to do with adults, separate from work with the child) to a more integrated 'central' location in the work carried out by the team, as follows:

**Periphery:** in some instances, obvious examples of physical violence were described by team members, but the case notes indicated that this violence was largely seen as an adult issue and remained a peripheral concern in terms of the work with the child. In such cases, therefore, the NSPCC team was deemed not to have identified domestic violence as an issue, even though there was awareness of its existence. In these instances it was *the researchers* who identified the existence of domestic violence.

**Centre:** those cases where domestic violence was identified by *the NSPCC team* as an issue were distinguished by it being seen as of central concern in order to understand the totality of the child's context, and in order to carry out any work with the child.

This issue of identification led to ongoing examination and discussions with the NSPCC team. Using the above parameters, cases judged to have been identified by the researchers or by the team as involving domestic violence were brought to the team meetings for discussion in

order to verify if the researchers were correct in these judgements. This served to validate the criteria whereby cases were evaluated as to their recognition of domestic violence as an issue by the NSPCC team.

# Increasing identification and integration of domestic violence

During the course of the research, domestic violence was increasingly being identified and integrated into the team's practice with children. This can be seen in a number of ways:

- an increase in the number and proportion of cases where the team rather than merely the researchers identified domestic violence as an issue;

- an increase in the actual number of words and detail used to describe and/or discuss domestic violence;

- the integration of domestic violence in the work carried out with children, as exemplified in the narratives.

These changes are discussed in more detail below.

## *Increase in cases where the team identified domestic violence as an issue*

As the project progressed, there was an increasing number of cases where the NSPCC team identified domestic violence as a central issue, and which they attempted to integrate into their practice in relation to children (see Table 2). In terms of the cases accepted for service in case file period A, eight of the total 59 cases were identified by the team as involving domestic violence. In case file period B this had

**Table 2: Accepted for service cases involving domestic violence as identified by the NSPCC team**

|  | DV identified by NSPCC team |
| --- | --- |
| Case file period A (total=59) | 8 (14%) |
| Case file period B (total=52) | 19 (37%) |
| Case file period C (total=22) | 7 (32%) |

**Table 3: Frequency of words and comments relating to domestic violence in case files from periods A and B**

| | Total words | Average words per case | Total comments | Average comments per case |
|---|---|---|---|---|
| Case file period A (total=29) | 3,056 | 105 | 138 | 4.8 |
| Case file period B (total=51) | 6,825 | 134 | 294 | 5.8 |

risen to 19 cases out of a total of 52 cases. In case file period C, seven out of the 22 cases accepted for service were seen to involve domestic violence. (It should be noted that the figures for case file period C reflects cases accepted for service over a six-month period, rather than a 12-month period as in A and B.)

*Increase in the number of words and detail used regarding domestic violence*

A quantitative content analysis of the data from the files showed an increase between case file periods A and B in the amount of narrative material extracted. This applied to both the number of words and the number of comments being used per case over the two time periods. In case file period A there were 3,056 words extracted in total, or an average of 105 words per case involving domestic violence (see Table 3). There was a total of 138 separate comments relating to domestic violence, or 4.8 comments on average per case.

In case file period B, by comparison, there was a total of 6,825 words extracted from the cases involving domestic violence, or an average of 133 words per case. There was a total of 294 separate comments, representing an average of 5.8 comments per case.

Across the case file periods, explicit information increasingly became apparent in the files about the different forms of abuse women experienced from their male partners. This indicated a change with regard to the specific details likely to be defined as domestic violence or abuse, and/or deemed of relevance by workers to note down in the files.

In both case file periods A and B, physical abuse to the woman/survivor of domestic violence was mentioned predominantly in relation to domestic violence. However, in case file period B other forms of abuse were also more likely to be recorded. Compared to the period before the project began (case file period A), there was in

**Figure 2: Forms of domestic violence identified (shown as percentage of total number of cases involving domestic violence in each period)**

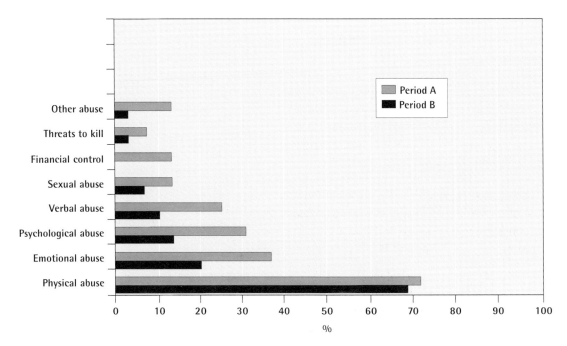

case file period B more than a two-fold increase in the identification of those cases where the violence also involved the sexual and/or verbal and/or psychological abuse of the woman. The existence of financial abuse was also mentioned for the first time. Although the numbers were small, in case file period B there were also more cases where there was mention of threats to kill.

The increase in the range of abusive behaviours identified as domestic violence across case file periods A and B is illustrated in Figure 2, which shows the percentage of the different forms of domestic violence within the total cases involving domestic violence in each period.

As the figure indicates, in case file period B there was an overall increase in the volume of information about domestic violence compared with the period before the project began. In the earlier case file A period, most of the cases involving domestic violence (17 out of the 29 cases or 58.6%) identified only *one* form of abuse as having occurred within the domestic violence context, usually physical. In case file period B, by contrast, over half the cases involving domestic violence (27 out of the 51 cases or 53%) were identified as having experienced between two and seven of the behaviours associated with domestic violence on the monitoring form.

In both case files periods A and B similar terminology was used to describe non-specific physically violent behaviour, as outlined in the 'violence/aggression' column in Table 1 on pp 19-20. However, in the case file period B case files there were more cases where more specific details were noted, such as those in the 'direct violence' column in the same table.

In addition to these obvious forms of physical abuse, files in both periods A and B contained references to what could be defined as behaviour that was abusive in a much broader sense. In the B files, however, there was a wider range of behaviours suggesting this form of abuse, and more specific examples given. Most of the behaviours listed in the 'controlling' and 'undermining' columns in Table 1 were found in the case file period B.

In the files in both periods there was relatively little mention of rape or sexual abuse as being a further aspect of the violence within these

relationships. In the A period files it was only apparent in two cases, where it was described as 'rape' in one instance and as 'sexual abuse' in the other. In the B period, sexual abuse featured more (in seven cases), because this was a specific category on the monitoring form. In the file commentary, however it was only mentioned in two instances. Thus, with regard to detail, this form of abuse appears to remain hidden, and not to be specifically noted down in the files.

There was also evidence to suggest that more consideration was beginning to be given to the effects of the domestic violence on the women concerned. In case file period A, the impact of violent/abusive behaviour was described only in relation to any physical injuries caused, whereas in case file period B some cases contained indications of some of the emotional impacts on women. The terminology used to describe these impacts can be seen in the 'impact on woman' column in Table 1.

### Integration of domestic violence in the work carried out with children

Examples of narrative taken from each of the three case file periods provided further evidence of how the issue of domestic violence was moving from the periphery to a more central and integrated feature of the work undertaken by the team.

In some of the case file period A files, for instance, the existence of domestic violence might be acknowledged by the team, but tended not to be explored in the work undertaken with the child:

> "[child, girl: 11] expressed negative feelings towards her father and was concerned about episodes of violence in her birth family.... I [NSPCC worker] am still unsure as to the nature and extent of the domestic difficulties which she [child] experienced in her birth family."

In this instance the child expressed anxiety in the initial NSPCC session about "her dad hitting my mum", but this disappeared from subsequent sessions where the focus was on the presenting issue of the sexual abuse of the child by the father. The connections, complexities and impact of the child's abusive experiences within the context of domestic violence were not addressed, and the worker did not attempt to gain details and information from the child to clarify the 'nature and extent of the domestic difficulties'. Domestic violence and the abuse of the child tended, thus, to be seen as separate issues.

In the case files in case file period B there are more examples of workers incorporating the domestic violence into the work with the child. For instance:

> "Mrs Green explained that when she was about 17 she had a partner who was violent towards her. Daisy [daughter now aged 11] was aged two at the time. Daisy said that she could remember instances from that time.... Daisy has informed Mrs Green that she has nightmares about her early years when Mrs Green had a violent partner.... Mrs Green and Daisy ... talked about how a violent relationship that Mrs Green was in when Daisy was one or two years old had impacted on both of them."

Again, in this example the presenting issue was child sexual abuse, but there is much more readiness to use the sessions to also explore past issues relating to domestic violence and to acknowledge the continuing impact of this for both mother and daughter. In this way, channels of communication were opened up between mother and daughter, and Daisy's current difficulties could be located within a wider context.

By the end of the project, in the cases in case file period C, acknowledgement of the interconnectedness of domestic violence and the safety and welfare of the child is integrated more

fully into practice in even more instances. For example, in one case accepted by the team, the presenting issue for the child, as reported by the mother, was the need to explore issues relating to the domestic violence the child had witnessed (rather than child sexual or physical abuse as in earlier cases). Exploring these issues then led to the discovery of the direct physical and sexual abuse of the child by her father:

> "Mrs Blue discussed that Lily [daughter aged 11] had witnessed the violence towards her mum. She [Lily] was threatened verbally and physically and was assaulted physically and verbally by her father.... Lily has told [mum] that she doesn't love her dad, but pretended to, to stop him from hurting Mrs Blue.... Lily has nightmares, cannot handle aggression in any form.... Cannot bear anyone to touch her."

Addressing the violence in this way, therefore, led to a greater awareness of the issues for the child in coping with the impact of both the direct abuse and the indirect abuse associated with living in the context of domestic violence. It also led to a greater awareness of the dynamics of the relationship between Lily and her mother, leading to more effective intervention with them both.

Thus, as the research project progressed, domestic violence moved from being a peripheral issue, which might sometimes emerge, to being a much more central feature of the team's work. Focusing on domestic violence in this way enabled the team to develop a wider contextual framework for the child's experiences. This applied both in those cases where domestic violence was the presenting issue and in those where there were other primary concerns.

# 5

# Disclosure and incidence of domestic violence

This chapter examines how involvement in the research project and the increasing focus on domestic violence led to changes in the team's general awareness and reported incidence of domestic violence. Issues and changes concerned with the disclosure of domestic violence are also discussed.

Findings from case file periods A and B, and the results from the monitoring exercise, are analysed in relation to these changes. Where relevant, there is also reference to the more limited data from the commentary material in case file period C. Analysis of the monitoring forms shows in particular how the use of, and detail in, these forms tended to reflect the general developments in the team with regard to the issue of domestic violence. Therefore, it is necessary first of all to look at the results of the use of the monitoring forms by the NSPCC team.

## The number of domestic violence monitoring forms completed by the team

During the total period of monitoring (that is, from the pilot monitoring phase beginning in December 1996 through to the end of the main monitoring period at the end of January 1998) a total of 45 cases included at least one completed client monitoring form. Information from these forms was collated both as a total and in relation to three separate points in the research. While recognising that these points in time were not strictly comparable, this was seen as useful in order to enable some charting of general trends or changes over time. Thus, the data from the

monitoring forms were examined at the following points:

- at the end of the pilot monitoring period (from December 1996 to the end of January 1997);

- at the end of case file period B (end of July 1997);

- at the end of case file period C (end of January 1998).

The numbers of cases with at least one completed monitoring form from each period were:

| | |
|---|---|
| **pilot monitoring** | 7 cases |
| **case file period B** | 26 cases |
| **case file period C** | 12 cases |

The numbers may appear relatively small, but it has to be recognised that a significant number of cases in case file period B were already open when the project began and therefore fell outside the parameters of the monitoring system. The fact that monitoring forms were not completed in *every* possible case is also indicative of the difficulties and time-span involved in introducing a new and systematised method into practice with a team which already had a well-established referral system (see Chapter 2) There were indications from the team that the completion of the monitoring forms was becoming increasingly systematic towards the end of the project.

Where monitoring forms were used, the majority of the cases contained only one form, though

**Figure 3: Number of monitoring forms per case**

Cases

Forms

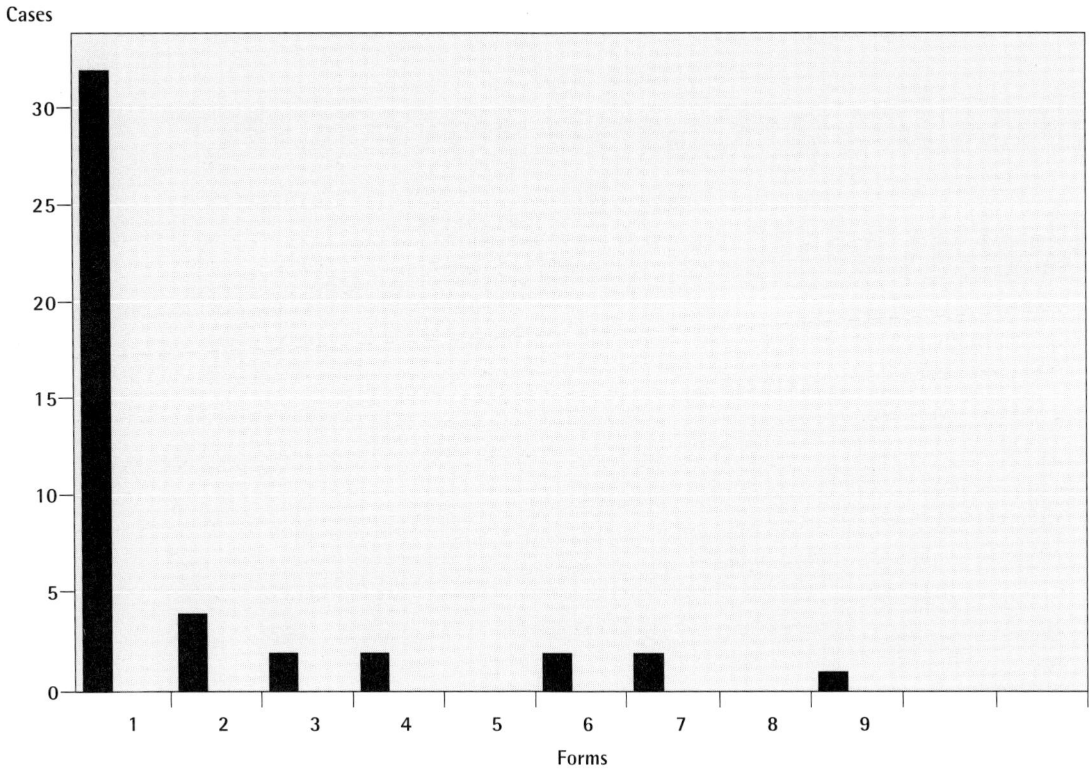

some contained more than one (see Figure 3). In total, 89 monitoring forms were completed.

As the research progressed there was evidence that the number of completed monitoring forms per case increased significantly, as follows:

| | |
|---|---|
| **pilot monitoring** | 11 forms in relation to 7 cases |
| **case file period B** | 37 forms in relation to 26 cases |
| **case file period C** | 41 forms in relation to 12 cases |

Indeed, six of the 13 cases which contained more than one monitoring form were found in the files in case file period C. Thus, over time as the team became more comfortable with domestic violence monitoring, and as the monitoring system became a more integrated aspect of the whole team, the forms were used more frequently.

## When was domestic violence disclosed?

There was evidence that the team's involvement in the research and the establishment of the monitoring scheme resulted in domestic violence

being identified as an issue from an earlier stage in the process.

In case file period A, for instance, there were 19 cases accepted for service which also involved domestic violence. Of these cases only four were clearly identified from the beginning of the NSPCC's involvement as including domestic violence. In contrast, in case file period B when domestic violence was being more routinely asked about at the point of referral and/or during the first direct contact with the service users, domestic violence was picked up by the team much earlier. Thus, of the 32 cases in case file period B which were accepted for service and which also involved domestic violence, in 14 of these the violence was identified from the beginning of the referral. This meant that all the issues in relation to the child could be assessed sooner, thereby leading to more effective intervention.

## Disclosure of domestic violence in case files

In those cases where domestic violence was identified across case file periods A and B the violence was mostly disclosed by the abused herself, although children, referrers and others

**Table 4: Source of disclosure of domestic violence (total and accepted for service cases involving domestic violence in case file periods A and B)**

| | Case file period A | | Case file period B | |
|---|---|---|---|---|
| | All cases with DV (total=29) | Accepted cases with DV (total=19) | All cases with DV (total=51) | Accepted cases with DV (total=32) |
| DV from abused | 14 (48.3%) | 11 (57.9%) | 29 (56.9%) | 22 (68.8%) |
| DV from child | 9 (31.0%) | 6 (31.6%) | 6 (11.8%) | 5 (15.6%) |
| DV from referrer | 6 (20.7%) | 1 (5.3%) | 20 (39.2%) | 10 (31.5%) |
| DV from other | 4 (13.8%) | 3 (15.8%) | 5 (9.8%) | 4 (12.5%) |

*Note: Totals are more than 100% because of disclosure by more than one source in some cases.*

also provided information about domestic violence. What did emerge was that during the period of the research the number of cases involving disclosure from children remained very similar, while there was a marked increase in disclosure from abused women themselves and from referrers. This can be partly explained by the fact that women were being asked specifically about experiences of domestic violence as a result of the monitoring process. Furthermore, knowledge about the project locally led to an increase in referrals concerning domestic violence. The increase in disclosure of domestic violence by women may also have decreased the need for children themselves to disclose the violence, especially as this was accompanied by domestic violence becoming a more central focus of the work with children.

This change in the pattern of disclosure held true across both case file periods A and B, whether looking at all the cases involving domestic violence or only those cases accepted for service involving domestic violence (see Table 4).

## Disclosure of domestic violence on monitoring forms

A similar pattern of disclosure emerged in the information from those cases involving domestic violence where a monitoring form had also been completed. The most frequently cited sources of disclosure on these forms were the abused woman herself (15 cases in total across all three time periods) and the referrer (nine cases in total across all time periods). In eight cases there was one more than one source of disclosure. However, as the research progressed there was

an increase in the number of cases where domestic violence emerged because the worker specifically asked about it.

There was evidence in a few cases of both disclosure and of specific details about the different forms of abuse experienced by the woman emerging over time as sessions progressed. In one example of this, the first form indicated that domestic violence was 'suspected'; the third form indicated 'don't know yet'; and the fourth form itemised seven forms of domestic violence experienced by the woman concerned – physical, sexual, psychological, emotional, verbal, threats to kill and isolation. This seems to confirm the fact noted by others (see, for example, Dobash and Dobash, 1992) that for some women disclosure of the violence they have experienced is both difficult, and will only occur over time. It is therefore important to consider domestic violence as a possibility, even when this does not immediately become apparent, and even when women are specifically asked about this but do not answer in the affirmative.

## Incidence of domestic violence in case files

As indicated in Chapter 4, all the files in case file periods A and B were examined in order to identify any references to domestic violence and to chart any changes in definition and volume of cases identified as domestic violence over time. Files in these periods were examined whether they were accepted for service cases or referred on or information/advice only cases.

**Table 5: Frequency of domestic violence across all types of cases in case file periods A and B**

| | Case file period A | | | Case file period B | | |
|---|---|---|---|---|---|---|
| | All cases (total=131) | Accepted for service cases (total=59) | Info/referred on cases (total=72) | All cases (total=136) | Accepted for service cases (total=52) | Info/referred on cases (total=84) |
| Cases with DV | 29 (22.1%) | 19 (32.2%) | 10 (13.9%) | 51 (37.5%) | 32 (61.5%) | 19 (22.6%) |

During case file periods A and B there was an almost two-fold increase in the total number of cases where domestic violence was identified, and more than a two-fold increase in the accepted for service cases involving domestic violence, as shown in Table 5.

The total figure in case file period B included one case where domestic violence was suspected and a further case where the possibility for violence was identified by the potential abuser himself. Neither of these cases was among the accepted for service cases involving domestic violence.

The increase in frequency did not necessarily mean that there had been an influx of domestic violence cases since the project started. While there appeared to be a small number of cases referred with domestic violence as the presenting issue – where mothers were wanting counselling for their children as a result of them living with violent partners, or other such support – the increase in number of domestic violence cases was primarily attributable to domestic violence being made more visible in the referrals for child abuse.

## Incidence of domestic violence on monitoring forms

Of the 45 cases with completed monitoring forms, domestic violence was identified in 26 cases, and in some cases was noted on more than one form. In other words, domestic violence was identified in over half (57.8%) of the cases where monitoring forms were completed. This figure was similarly consistent across all three time periods. This suggests that monitoring forms tended to be used more frequently when there was evidence of domestic violence from early on in a case.

Twenty-two of the 26 cases with monitoring forms indicating the existence of domestic violence, identified physical violence as a component of this. In eight of these cases there was mention of physical violence to the exclusion of all other possible forms of violence, while 13 of the cases identified a range of between three and seven abusive behaviours as being part of the context of the violence. It is worth noting that there was evidence by the end of the research of some change in the team's recognition and understanding of the more generally abusive behaviours. In the monitoring forms relating to case file period C, none of the cases involving domestic violence was identified as exclusively consisting of physical violence, and where details were known (in six of the seven cases), all identified a range of three or more behaviours as being part of an overall abusive situation.

The data from the pilot and case file period B monitoring forms were compared to similar data from the case files. The data were comparable in terms of the existence of domestic violence in all but three instances. In the latter three cases there was a contradiction about domestic violence in the sense that it was identified by the researchers as being an issue, but no domestic violence was indicated by the NSPCC team on the monitoring form. On a further three forms, the abuse to the child was itemised in the part of the form relating to the experience of the adults, thus moving beyond the agreed definition of domestic violence, and leading to confusion as to who was involved.

A similar comparison was not possible in relation to case file period C as not all the case files in this period were examined by the researchers, as explained earlier. Of the files in this period identified by the team on the monitoring form as involving domestic violence, there was one example of some continuing confusion over the definition of domestic violence. This was a case where abusive behaviour from a child to his mother had been identified as domestic violence by a member of the NSPCC team.

## Who was being violent to whom

The case files examined in periods A and B were identical with regard to the genders of the perpetrator and the abused, with domestic violence always having involved violence from a man to his female partner, either currently or in the past. This pattern was also replicated in the more limited data available from the files in case file period C.

However, the language used (see Table 1 in Chapter 4) could at times mask this male to female direction of the violence. For instance, in two of the 29 cases in case file period A there was a suggestion that the violence was mutually 'to each other'. In other cases the violence was described at times as 'fighting', suggesting some form of mutuality, although this may not have been intentional.

In case file period B there were four cases where there was mention of the woman also 'hitting' or 'assaulting' the man, either in retaliation to his verbal abuse or as the result of 'arguments' between them. In one case this 'fracas' had resulted in the woman being arrested, and in another the woman was on probation for 'offences of affray'. Although 'fighting' was not used in case file period B to describe any of the violence, there were two cases where terminology used to describe the violence suggested some degree of mutuality. In one case, for instance, there was reference to a "very violent relationship *between* the parents", although there was nothing in the documentation to suggest that the woman was also violent. In another case the woman described being belittled by her male partner, and unable to express her views in his presence. It was agreed that a joint meeting would be

inappropriate and that any work with the parents would be difficult because the worker "felt that each parent would be undermining each other", again suggesting, perhaps unintentionally, some form of reciprocation.

Most of the cases involving domestic violence concerned current or previous violence in the relationship of the parents/parent figures of the child who was the subject of the referral. In case file period A there were also three cases of domestic violence in the current or previous relationships of women who were themselves known to be survivors of childhood sexual abuse, one case where domestic violence was identified in the woman's current relationship and also between her parents when she was a child, and one case of domestic violence between the parents of the young woman (aged 16) referred and also in her own relationships.

In case file period B, in five cases there had been violence in more than one of the mother's relationships. Two of these included previous violence from male partners as well as violence from the mother's current/previous female partner(s). Another case involved domestic violence between the parents of an adult survivor of childhood sexual abuse. A further case (already discussed in relation to reframing in Chapter 3) could be defined as both domestic violence and child abuse, as it involved violence and sexual abuse towards a young woman (16) who was in a relationship with an adult man in a position of authority over her. In case file periods B and C there was also one example in each period of domestic violence having occurred in the previous generation, namely from the grandfather to the grandmother of the children who had been referred to the team.

In addition, from both the case files and from the monitoring forms there were indications of the ways in which children were implicated in the dynamics of domestic violence. There was also some evidence of the possible effects on children of living with domestic violence. These findings will be discussed in the following chapter.

# 6

# Domestic violence and children

This chapter examines the findings from the case files and from the monitoring forms relating to children's experiences of domestic violence. It will also explore the possible detrimental effects of this on the children concerned. Findings from the files are mostly drawn from case file periods A and B, with some additional commentary material from the files in case file period C. Comparison of the findings from the different periods of time serves to further chart the changes in the team's attitudes and awareness of domestic violence as the research progressed.

As will be detailed below, in the cases where domestic violence was identified, the perpetrator of the domestic violence and the abuser of the child(ren) was likely to be the same individual. The generally abusive impact on children, both 'indirect' and 'direct', of living in circumstances of domestic violence was also apparent.

These findings are consistent with a range of other research which has found links between child abuse and domestic violence (Humpreys, 1997; Brandon and Lewis, 1996; Farmer and Owen, 1995; Forman, 1995; Goddard and Hiller, 1993). They also confirm the findings of other studies, which have shown the range of detrimental effects on children of living with domestic violence (McGee, forthcoming; Abrahams, 1994; Jaffe et al, 1990). Also evident in the cases involving domestic violence was the complex dynamics of survival and protection that both children and their mothers engage in where men are violent, which again has been replicated in other research (for an overview, see Hester et al, 1998).

It is important to note that the detailed sample of 111 accepted for service cases in this study is

similar in size to previous studies into children with child protection concerns carried out in the UK, and indeed larger than some of these (see Maynard, 1985; Cleaver and Freeman, 1995; Farmer and Owen, 1995; Brandon and Lewis, 1996; Glaser and Prior, 1997; Humphreys, 1997; and Gibbons et al, 1995).

Moreover, the cases examined in this study provide a wider sample. Other studies have tended to focus on children with social services involvement, or on women and children in refuges. In this study there was social services involvement in relation to less than three quarters of the children (72.9%) in cases accepted for service in case file period A and less than half of the children (48.9%) in cases accepted for service in period B. A small number of these children and their mothers were also, or had been, staying at a refuge.

All the cases, including those involving domestic violence, contained more girls than boys as service users (see Table 6). In case file period B there were an additional two children whose gender was not indicated.

## Domestic violence and the sexual/ physical/emotional abuse of children (case files)

The referral forms used by the NSPCC ask for only one main concern to be identified in relation to the child. What follows is an analysis of the findings regarding these main categories of abuse. Where relevant, additional information about further forms of abuse to the children is also included, which has been identified from

**Table 6: Gender (where known) of children in the cases involving domestic violence**

|  | Case file period A (total=44) | Case file period B (total=81) |
| --- | --- | --- |
| Girls | 29 (65.9%) | 47 (58%) |
| Boys | 15 (34.1%) | 34 (42%) |

the commentary material in the files. In reality the forms of abuse are not mutually exclusive, and children often suffered an overlapping range of physical, sexual and emotional abuse.

*Sexual abuse*

Across case file periods A and B, a detailed examination was undertaken of all the cases which cited sexual abuse as the main focus of concern for the child. As the team specialised in treatment/recovery work with survivors of sexual abuse such work featured prominently, especially in the cases accepted for service (see Appendix B, Table 4).

In case file period A, in both the total and accepted for service case files, a wide range of child sexual abusers was identified, including immediate and extended family members (such as fathers, brothers, uncles, grandfathers), strangers and peers. In some cases there had been abuse by more than one person. In all but one case (involving an allegation of abuse by the male and female foster parents) the abusers were male. Similarly, in case file period B there was a range of child sexual abusers in the total and accepted for service samples, including immediate and extended family members, and also non-family members, such as neighbours, family friends, peers and a few strangers. In all but two cases the abusers were male, and in another case both parents were cited as the abusers. Generally, across both case period A and B, fathers or father figures (that is, partners, step-parents and cohabitees, etc) constituted nearly half of the abusers in the cases accepted for service, and were the largest single group identified as perpetrators of child sexual abuse (21 of 44 cases in A [47.7%]; 18 of 39 in B [46.2%]).

In comparison, the cases with sexual abuse as the main concern but which also involved domestic violence, featured a narrower range of perpetrators of sexual abuse against children. In

particular, the proportion of fathers or father figures who had sexually abused their children was higher in these cases (9 of 14 in period A [64.3%]; 13 of 23 in period B [56.5%]). Moreover, all of these fathers or father figures were also the domestic violence perpetrators.

For the team, being made aware of these patterns in the cases they dealt with was important in relation to their practice. Such evidence helped them to work more realistically with children and their carers where domestic violence was also a part of their experience. Realising that for some children their abuser was also violent to the mothers, and vice versa, led to greater understanding of the abusive dynamics experienced by the children concerned. It also meant that in the few instances where mothers contacted the NSPCC regarding support for their children who had lived in circumstances of domestic violence, team members became more open to the possibility that the children had been directly abused in addition to witnessing violence to their mothers. Case files in period C indicated that, as a consequence, work was being carried out with children on this wider range of abusive experiences.

From the commentary material across all three case file periods there was also evidence of the close interaction between the man's sexual abuse of the child and the physical/emotional/sexual abuse of the mother. This involved the male partner using threats of physical abuse and threats to kill the mother and/or the child in order to secure the child's silence about his sexual abuse of her/him. This may be seen to add an additional level of emotional abuse to children who in this way became responsible for their own and their mother's safety.

*Physical abuse*

In 21 cases across case file periods A and B, there was also mention of physical abuse to children being committed by the perpetrator of the domestic violence. Some of these cases involved physical abuse as the focus of concern, and in others the link between the physical abuse of children in a domestic violence context was noted in the commentary material, even though this was not the primary reason for referral.

### Emotional abuse

Across all the cases in case file periods A and B, emotional abuse was very rarely cited as the focus of concern (see Appendix B, Table 4). This was especially true of the cases in period A where it featured in only 2.3% (total=3) of the total cases and not at all in either the accepted for service or domestic violence cases. Although the numbers were still small, in period B emotional abuse was the primary concern in a higher number of the total files, and three quarters (8 out of 12) of these cases also appeared in the domestic violence sample. This represented a slight change in focus by the team, and was partly a reflection of changes in the kinds of referrals coming through to the team resulting from participation in the research. However, not all cases involving the emotional abuse of children living with domestic violence were considered within the remit of the team's work.

In case file period C, three of the seven cases involving domestic violence mention the emotional abuse experienced by the child in this context, although it is not known whether any of these cases identified this emotional abuse as the main focus of the referral.

It is clear that, during case file period B, cases of children witnessing domestic violence began to be labelled as emotional abuse. Emphasising emotional abuse as a consequence of the child living with domestic violence appeared to suggest that such abuse of children was merely an unintended effect. However, the narrative from the period B files also indicated some instances where the emotional abuse of the child was probably a deliberate act against the children. This included one case where the children were shut in a room with their mother while she was being beaten by her male partner. In this same case the older boy (aged six at the time) was later blamed by the man for the injuries he had caused the mother. In another

example the man was threatening suicide and cutting himself in front of his children in order to 'prove' his wish to be reconciled with his ex-wife.

## Domestic violence and the sexual/physical/emotional abuse of children (monitoring forms)

Some of the monitoring forms which had identified the existence of domestic violence also made mention of the direct and indirect abuse of children within this context. This was evident in a total of 10 cases, of which seven made reference to children being physically hit. In two of these cases there was also physical violence to other siblings in the family. In another three there was mention of additional abuse to the child(ren) from the same man, which included one child who had been sexually abused, another who was subjected to 'low warmth' and other children experiencing threats to kill. The remaining three cases involved threats to the child, emotional abuse (in the form of 'low warmth and much criticism') and sexual abuse, which was described as the child being "doubly abused – sexually and saw mum being abused".

Such details on the monitoring forms regarding the interconnectedness of different forms of abuse of children by the domestic violence perpetrator appeared more frequently as the research progressed. This suggests that further details about children emerged as the team became more confident in asking about and dealing with domestic violence.

## The impact on children of living with domestic violence (case files)

Because children were mostly referred to the NSPCC team for reasons other than domestic violence (although referrals explicitly concerning this were beginning to occur in periods B and C), there was some difficulty when examining the files in separating out the possible effects for children of living with/witnessing domestic violence from the possible effects of their other abusive experiences. This issue was explored in interviews and discussions with the team. Despite these difficulties, in case file periods A

**Table 7: Impact of domestic violence on children as noted by researchers or by NSPCC team**

| | Case file period A cases with domestic violence (total=29) | Case file period B cases with domestic violence (total=51) |
| --- | --- | --- |
| DV impact on child noted by researchers | 18 (62.1%) | 24 (47.1%) |
| DV impact on child noted by NSPCC team | 7 (24.1%) | 16 (31.4%) |

and B, between almost a half and two thirds of cases contained some reference to an emotional or behavioural impact on the child(ren) which appeared to be linked to their experiences of living with domestic violence.

As the researchers examined the case files in periods A and B for evidence of effects on children, an assessment was made as to whether these effects were also identified by the NSPCC team. In some cases this assessment was based on direct references being made to some such detrimental effect, or children themselves making (implicit or explicit) connections between their own behaviour and what they had experienced. In other cases the impact was noted by the team in the sense that this became part of the focus of subsequent work, or was clearly part of supervision or discussion of the case, or was raised as an issue with other professionals involved.

In comparison to case file period A, in case file period B there was a notable increase in identification by the team of the impacts on children (see Table 7). It appeared that focusing to a greater extent on the identification of domestic violence also increased awareness of the impact of this on children, and vice versa.

There was evidence from the commentary material across all three case file periods of the wide range of experiences children had of living with domestic violence, with the files in case file period B containing a greater volume of information on this aspect. The emotional impact on children of witnessing domestic violence also tended to be made much more explicit in these files. Effects might occur whether children were directly abused themselves and/or were witnesses to the domestic violence. The range of children's reactions was complex and contradictory (presumably affected to some extent by factors

such as age, gender, the form and frequency of the violence and how long children were living in such a situation – see Hester et al, 1998).

Across all sets of files, several children were described as having witnessed attacks of physical violence towards their mothers. In case file period A this included one instance of the child witnessing her mother being stabbed in the head, while others were also witnesses to the after-effects of violence in the form of their mother's black eyes and broken bones. Case file period B included two cases where children saw their mothers being attacked with knives, and in one of these instances the two children also witnessed their mother being strangled. In this latter example the older child, a boy aged five, was said to have "just stood there while it happened". Within case file period C, there was a further example of a child witnessing her father putting a knife to her mother's throat.

Some children remembered the violence even though their mothers did not realise that they had been aware of it. One older child recounted the violence she had witnessed as a much younger child (aged two or three), and in another instance a five-year-old daughter used the first interview session with the NSPCC "to recount unprompted memories from the past of abuse ... that she observed and which ... [mother] remembers but never thought [daughter] had seen".

In the cases with domestic violence, throughout the research period there were children who were reported as having tried various methods to try and protect their mothers. Whether made explicit or not, trying to intervene or protect mothers could carry physical risks for children, or could potentially overburden them with an adult sense of responsibility to stop the abuse. In case file period A, this attempt at protection included physically intervening in the violence

33

or withholding information which the children knew might lead to a violent attack on their mother. Others ran out of the house to try and get help when violence was occurring, even though they were 'hysterical' themselves. One child requested a weapon to take home with him from his session at the NSPCC so that he could kill the man who was being physically violent to his mother, and thereby protect her from any further abuse. Similarly, a son (aged 17) was described as sleeping with a baseball bat in order to protect himself and his mother in case his father came to the house, and a 12-year-old expressed a desire to kill his mother's abusive partner. In another example, a 15-year-old daughter had tried to physically intervene between her mother and her mother's partner when they were having an 'argument', which had resulted in the partner chasing the daughter and attempting to strangle her. One daughter (aged 11) described how she pleaded for her mother's safety whenever her father had a knife to her mother's throat.

The cases with domestic violence also contained other examples where the effect on the child appeared to be linked to their living with domestic violence. Two boys (aged eight and six) who had witnessed their mother being attacked with a knife had both subsequently "acted out with knives". The reaction of some children was the opposite of this 'acting out' aggression in that they became withdrawn and retreated to the safety of their room, and/or felt frightened and silenced. In case file period A, one young child expressed his fear that he was going to be beaten up "like mummy", and in case file period B, a seven-year-old daughter was said to be fearful that their father "could kill them all". In case file period C, one 11-year-old girl was variously described as having nightmares, scared of the dark, frightened of loud noises, having temper tantrums, being 'uncontrollable' and self-harming. This behaviour was seen by the team to be the result of the child witnessing violence to her mother, coupled with experiencing physical abuse from her father.

One mother had placed her children in care because she perceived this as the best means of protecting her children from further domestic violence. In period B one mother was 'harassed' to such an extent that she escaped from the house, but had to leave the children in the care of the father. In another case in case file period

B, there was recognition that children were "exhibiting major problems as a result of living with domestic violence", and that these were compounded by the fact that the violence had necessitated many changes of address and brought much uncertainty.

## The impact on children of living with domestic violence (monitoring forms)

Analysis of the monitoring forms across the period of the research provided evidence of the NSPCC team's growing awareness and confidence in recognising the effects of domestic violence on children. This was particularly so in relation to the effects of witnessing abuse and/or of children 'acting out' in an aggressive manner.

At the start of the research, team members were unsure whether it was possible to determine the specific impacts of domestic violence on children, especially as they were working with children who had usually also experienced other forms of abuse. The problem was discussed in relation to the monitoring forms, which included a question on the effects of domestic violence on the child. The difficulties were highlighted by the fact that only one of the pilot monitoring forms (out of three cases involving domestic violence) made any reference to an impact of domestic violence on a child, in terms of the child 'hitting out'.

During case file period B, there were indications in many more cases that domestic violence might be having an impact on children. Of the 16 cases identified on the monitoring forms in this period as involving domestic violence, 11 indicated that there had been an impact for the children. Where details were given, these included children being scared or frightened and/or being aggressive or angry towards their mothers. In one case more details of the effects were provided, including the child being 'unpleasant/violent to his sister', being 'blamed for the violence' and having 'attachment problems'. In two of these cases there was evidence that details of the impact on the child emerged as sessions progressed.

By case file period C, almost all the cases with domestic violence included mention of an impact on the child on the monitoring form. This applied to six of the seven cases identified as involving domestic violence. Two cited a range of effects on the child, including having nightmares, destroying a bedroom, keeping a knife for protection, and learning to keep feelings inside. Again, in three of these cases, details emerged over time.

While the numbers are too small to make generalisations, the monitoring forms do appear to reflect a change in the team in terms of the identification of the effects on children of living with domestic violence.

## Domestic violence and post-separation contact as a context for the abuse of children

Difficulties arising from children's residence or contact arrangements appeared regularly in the close examination of the files in case file periods A and B. Such problems were especially linked to the domestic violence context. Between two thirds and three quarters of the cases where there were contact/residence difficulties also involved domestic violence (that is, in case file period A, 12 out of 17 total cases [70.6%]; in case file period B, 21 out of 30 total cases [70%] – see Table 8).

Cases involving domestic violence were more likely to involve problems concerning residence, and especially contact, than in the sample as a whole. Echoing previous research (Hester and Radford, 1996), it was the potential or actual abuse of children during contact, the need for supervised contact, and the potential for a

conflict of interests between the mother and child(ren), which were the main concerns.

A closer examination of the domestic violence narrative material across all three case file periods gave some further indications as to the nature of some of the concerns regarding contact or residence in situations of domestic violence. There was a clear overlap between the existence of domestic violence and the abuse of children during contact, whether physical, sexual or emotional.

In case file period C, the team were involved in a particularly harrowing case where there were problems with contact in a context of domestic violence. The team were providing counselling to a child whose father had been violent and abusive to both his partner and his daughter prior to the separation of the parents. The father was in the process of trying to change his supervised contact with both his daughters to unsupervised contact. During the course of sessions with the NSPCC and in discussions with her mother, the child gradually disclosed that her father was physically abusing her and her sister during the supervised contact by "playing hitting games". She also disclosed violence to her sister from her father prior to the separation. This was followed by a disclosure of sexual abuse happening to both girls during the supervised contact. The daughter expressed fears about having contact with her father, often through her 'wild' and self-harming behaviour after contact, leading the NSPCC to recommend there should be no contact. Despite this, the court ordered that supervised contact should continue.

## Table 8: Frequency of contact/residence issues

| | Case file period A | | | Case file period B | | |
|---|---|---|---|---|---|---|
| | All cases (total=131) | Accepted for service cases (total=59) | Cases with domestic violence (total=29) | All cases (total=136) | Accepted for service cases (total=52) | Cases with domestic violence (total=51) |
| Contact residence issues | 17 (13% of all cases) | 11 (18.6% of accepted for service cases) | 12 (41.4% of all cases with dv) | 30 (22.1% of all cases) | 20 (38.5% of accepted for service cases) | 21 (41.2% of all cases with dv) |

# 7

# The impact on practice in relation to children

This chapter considers how involvement in the research, and the incorporation of domestic violence into the NSPCC team's work, led to changes in its practice, including more effective abuse prevention work with children.

We have already outlined many of the general changes apparent in the team's work once the project was underway, including the shift of focus on domestic violence from the periphery to the core of the work in relation to children. This change of focus also had a direct impact on the way in which team members worked with clients. Overall, team members felt that focusing on domestic violence had enhanced their abuse prevention work with children (it would be useful to assess service users' perspectives in the longer term as well, but that was only possible in a few cases within the time-scale of the project). A number of themes regarding the impact on the team's practice emerged from the interviews with team members, including the effect on referrals, practice with children and their parents, interagency work and new problem areas which the work revealed for the team.

## Increase and change in referrals

Chapter 5 indicated the general increase in cases being identified as involving domestic violence. From the interviews it was apparent that there had been a small increase in the number of referrals where domestic violence and the resultant impact on children was the presenting issue. Some of these were labelled as 'emotional abuse' on the referral form due to the lack of a box to tick for domestic violence. These referrals appeared to be largely due to people

hearing about the project and due to the networking which had resulted from this:

"I think people out there have heard that we're doing this research and I think because of the links with the research and talking with the outside world, you know, the networking a bit more."

This increase had created some anxiety and concern that the perceived change in the type and threshold of abuse cases being accepted by the team would lead to an opening of the 'floodgates', to which the team would have difficulty in responding. It may be that, in some instances, the team would be largely dealing with the same cases, but with a differently identified presenting issue. However, the team also clearly felt that there were some cases accepted during the period of the research which would not have been accepted for service prior to the research because they involved domestic violence. In this way, involvement in the research allowed the team to incorporate a wider range of child abuse in their work, in that the very fact of living with domestic violence was being seen as abusive to children. It therefore became an important and relevant issue to work with in practice.

Some members of the team felt somewhat overwhelmed by the new work they were encountering, although they were responding positively to the change:

"I mean, I'm feeling a bit overwhelmed at the moment by the amount of stuff coming in, not being able to respond to it quickly enough. But then, you know, if I'm able to reflect and I'm able to be more optimistic ... at least we know that's the need, then you can ... then it's partly our responsibility to create ways of meeting that."

## Impact on awareness of the issues

Individual team members felt by the end of the research project that they had a much better understanding of the issues concerning domestic violence and the relevance for children. As one team member explained:

"I suppose I went along with the – not consciously – with the view that ... domestic violence ... was kind of in a compartment on its own, like the police used to think don't interfere with domestic violence.... That was the culture. Don't get involved in domestics ... your instant thought is, or mine was, why did you stay? Until you understand the kind of dynamics ... although I know ... what the power dynamics are in the circumstances, you don't automatically think about it in terms of domestic violence – or I didn't. So I suppose, yes, I now ... I would ask it now when I first see somebody – I'm happy to and will continue to do so."

The project had also made it easier for those who already considered that living with domestic violence was an important aspect for some children to voice those concerns, and discuss them with the whole team.

From the interviews and team meetings it was apparent that there continued to be ongoing debates among workers about what to incorporate in a definition of domestic violence. A major concern was whether it is exclusively violence to adults or violence and abuse 'in the family' generally. Another aspect of the debates was the way in which living in a context of domestic violence impacted on children.

As outlined in Chapter 6, the case files indicated that domestic violence perpetrators and abusers of children were often the same individuals, and that children may be directly sexually and/or physically abused by their fathers or father figures who were also abusing the mothers.

Recognition of this overlap became an important issue for the team's practice. Yet there was also a tendency for team members to see domestic violence purely as an emotional abuse for children (in the sense of living in a violent environment) and thus separate from the sexual or physical abuse of children. In other words, if domestic violence was the presenting issue, emotional abuse of the children would be seen as the potential problem rather than other, direct forms of child abuse. As one member of staff put it:

"... that's been the most major thing I suppose; it's changed our remit in some way from just sexual abuse to domestic violence. It seems to be two remits now – children who've been sexually abused and children who have experienced domestic violence, or though there may be other...."

This was perhaps not surprising, as the team expected sexual abuse and physical abuse of the children to be the presenting issue, and not domestic violence, even if domestic violence might be in the background in these instances.

However, taking the 'emotional abuse' line was seen to have potential problems in relation to thresholds of abuse accepted for intervention by social services:

"... it's a difficult one because I'm not sure that, if you didn't have anything else, ie, other sorts of abuse, my guess is social workers wouldn't do it.... And what would that social worker do? Would they go out and run an investigation? OK, they'd do that and what have, you know, would that be the best thing for the woman?.... Would it make the woman safer, and what would you do if the woman didn't leave or the man didn't leave? Would you say to the man he had to leave? Would the new legislation back you in that?"

Despite this area of tension, the team all felt by the end of the project that thinking about domestic violence, and incorporating these issues into practice with the child, meant that children were better protected. It provided a further indication of possible harm to the child and another factor with regard to problematic behaviour. For example:

"We look at domestic violence in terms of danger to children as you would if a child was hit. Do you know what I mean? It's quite hard to explain isn't it! But it's – apart from saying it's there on the agenda very clearly now, for me it is looked at as you would look at a child who has a bruise.... Are these children safe in a situation where say they're not necessarily being hit themselves but there is a high level of violence in the family – are they safe? What support is that person or that woman getting? And I suppose I would hope that if there were problems with the children, that agencies, including ourselves would not – and I hope, I'm sure they wouldn't, hope they wouldn't – automatically think that it's the child that's the problem. So I think too that for me where there is a referral of a child that has problematic behaviour, domestic violence is one of the issues that I would be considering along with sexual abuse or emotional abuse or physical abuse, for an explanation of that behaviour."

This represented a huge change in practice and awareness from this worker, who at the beginning of the project had seen domestic violence in its own separate 'compartment'.

## Practice with children and their parents

Team members talked about a variety of ways in which incorporating domestic violence into their work had enhanced their practice. One aspect concerned a greater understanding of the overlap in the dynamics of both child abuse and domestic violence. For instance, that both domestic violence and child abuse concern the exertion of power and control by one person over another. Thinking about these similarities had enabled the team to reflect more thoroughly on their use of particular approaches:

"But actually the similarities with sexual abuse are more than they are dissimilar ..., because it seems to me it's about power and control still again."

Thus, having a practice framework that included an understanding of domestic violence was generally seen to enhance practice and partnership work with parents. It allowed a better understanding of what was going on in many of the cases:

"... this framework of domestic violence that explains a lot to us – it explains a lot of people's actions, or could help to explain them, ... I think it can only help us work in partnership much better."

It had led the team to work with both mothers and their children in domestic violence cases, and that was considered especially positive for all concerned:

"... if a child has been abused, it's what happens next in terms of the help, of an acceptance from particular key carers. That it's the quality of that that will determine the outcome in terms of the child's recovery.... So, therefore, if we can work with women as well as children, carers as well as children, taking account of domestic violence ... in other words, if we have an understanding of some of the power dynamics around, and the frequency with which men abuse women we know about just in a factual way, then I think that we can start to create with those carers safer environments for them and their children."

Moreover:

"... if we've got some more information and more experience and more knowledge about the kinds of scenarios that flow from women suffering domestic violence, I think we'll be in a better position again, you know, not to rush to make inappropriate judgements or feed inappropriate beliefs or rush into inappropriate action, like sort of removing children or put them on registers or whatever it might be ... if we start creating safer and more open frameworks by talking, you know – by not talking about, 'well, this woman dumped this child somewhere', we say that this woman had to leave this child because we understood the tremendous pressure she was under and she was having to make very difficult choices, or whatever it was."

Across case periods A and B it was clear that in cases involving domestic violence the team were more likely to work with the mother and child together in a session than in those where domestic violence was not deemed to be an issue. Mothers were also more likely to be seen separately as part of the work with the child in the cases involving domestic violence.

## The user perspective

From the outset of the research it was intended to examine the user evaluation forms returned by clients after work with the NSPCC had ended. Alongside the incorporation of domestic violence as an issue in the team's work with abused children, an additional question regarding domestic violence had also been added to the evaluation form. Unfortunately, the return rate for the user evaluation forms was generally very low, and forms from only three families which included the question specifically about domestic violence were returned within the research period.

From the very small number of completed service user evaluation forms, it was apparent that being asked about domestic violence was useful, even though painful at times for the women and children concerned. One woman wrote that it had helped her to realise she was not alone in her experiences, while a child had noted how frightened she felt that "somebody would get me" because she had broken the secrecy surrounding her experiences. This confirms the need for the skilful handling of disclosures by both women and children.

## 'Systemic' practice

The team started out seeing a systemic approach as a way of incorporating the experiences of the adults as well as the children. By the end of the project they had many examples of how their particular 'systemic' approach was positive in domestic violence cases:

> "Sometimes it's quite clear that domestic violence is the biggest ingredient in the whole problem, and I, with that particular woman – looking at it systemically again, living in our society where women are not treated in equal

way to males, and then her particular family where that pattern was repeated; and then growing up, getting married and the sort of places that she had to be, the culture she had to live in, again reinforced that whole sort of attitude. And then you can see why it was so easy for the sexual abuse to take place in the context of domestic violence which had made her appear to the rest of the family – the children, and herself – inferior, to blame. And then, of course, mothers who have children who are sexually abused get the blame and blame themselves, so, looking at the blame, you had to look at the domestic violence aspect of it because it was such a prime mover."

The project had also brought to the fore team members' critique of traditional family therapy approaches. Incorporating issues concerning domestic violence had shown (yet again) that everyone in the family was not affected equally, and that responsibility for the abuse had to be placed with the abuser:

> "It's very difficult to work in a purely systemic way with families where there've been those things happening because, you know, I don't believe that they're – you know, everybody equally, affects the other person. I think it is totally unethical to say that."

> "... whilst I might, because working with a couple – you know, where there's been domestic violence – I might be interested in the patterns that he'd experienced, and, you know, how it happened to him, whether he'd been physically abused or sexually abused, whatever, why he believed it was ... you know, what his beliefs were and all that. You have to explore that. But I also have to say, *you* are responsible for this, you know, and your actions, and that the woman and the children were not responsible for it in any way.... There are sort of sometimes ways in which you can help a family if they're really committed to stopping the abuse. Then you can actually look at patterns of behaviour and look at a sort of ... the reciprocal sort of nature of things. That can make a difference. But you have to

know that the person who is the abuser is actually really dedicated and how many are there of those around."

## Interagency links

We examined how far other agencies and professionals were involved with families seeking a service from the NSPCC. These included social services departments, the family court welfare and probation services, the police, Women's Aid, solicitors, the health service and education departments (the latter in some more specific way other than children attending school). Agencies were identified as being involved in the lives of children and families if they had some current active responsibility for families.

Across case file periods A and B, the most significant agency involved was social services, although this was less so in case file period B. In case file period A, there was social services involvement in 44.3% (n=58) of the total requests for service cases, or 72.9% (n=43) of the accepted for service cases, and 65.5% (n=19) of the domestic violence sample. In case file period B, social services were involved in 35.3% (n=48) of the total requests, 48.1% (n=25) of those cases accepted for service, and 47.1% (n=24) of the cases involving domestic violence.

In both case file periods A and B, the remaining professionals and agencies were involved very infrequently, although some of the cases might have had more police involvement, for instance, at the point of disclosure of the abuse. Despite the difficulties with contact and residence in the cases involving domestic violence, relatively few cases had court welfare or solicitor involvement.

Team members expressed concern that where other agencies such as social services were involved in domestic violence cases, mothers and children might be seen and worked with entirely separately by different agencies. They felt that this led to less effective work overall, and they would themselves have preferred to work with mother and child together, or to work very closely with the other agency. This was obviously going to be an issue of ongoing debate and concern for the team. For example:

"It just does worry me about how we're going to work together with social

services. That's what worries me actually – working together with social services to enable protection of the children to be looked at properly, whilst ensuring that the children and the mother are safe at the same time...."

Members of the team pointed out that involvement in the project had led them to increase their links with other agencies. This was particularly so in relation to those agencies and organisations working with women and children who were or had been living in circumstances of domestic violence. This was seen as a generally positive development:

"... it's so important to work with other agencies like domestic violence help lines and projects, and also with the refuges. That's something that it's done, it has actually brought more people together."

For instance, the local ACPC (Area Child Protection Committee) had held a conference on domestic violence and the team had presented some of the interim findings from the research at this.

Generally it was felt by the team that their increasing interagency links were positive in terms of crossing some of the boundaries between statutory and voluntary agencies, with the result that children could be given a better service and perhaps be more protected in the longer term:

"[the project has] led me ... to meet with and talk to and listen to a range of very different people, ranging from the family advice line to the Black and Asian minority community ... so it's taken us away from statutory SSD, if you like, and any other recognised child protection agencies and the police ... it's just had a terrific impact on how we see families and how we see children."

A domestic violence forum had been established locally, and the team were involved in this. It had been useful to have these links in order to obtain and share information about domestic violence, and also to see where and how to refer women and children if or when it was inappropriate or not possible for the NSPCC to accept a referral for service.

# 8

# Conclusion

The project set out with the aim of examining how professionals from an NSPCC team, working with abused children, might incorporate the issue of domestic violence into their practice, and the impact of doing this. A monitoring scheme for domestic violence was developed to be used in all referrals and in relation to every session of work with service users. The mechanism of reframing was also used to introduce the issue of domestic violence into work with abused children.

The team did not find it easy to implement the monitoring scheme, and it was especially difficult for the forms to be used systematically in every case and in every session. The client-centred methods of working compounded these difficulties. The implementation of the monitoring scheme was aided by the administration staff adding the forms to the existing referral and case recording forms used by the team, and thereby integrating the use of monitoring within the team's existing systems. By the end of the project there were indications that the completion of the monitoring forms was becoming increasingly systematic and that the team had found the use of monitoring very positive overall.

The team found the use of reframing particularly useful. This enabled them to work through previous and current cases in order to see what would happen if the issue of domestic violence was incorporated.

As the project progressed, there was a clear change within the team, both in relation to awareness of domestic violence issues and in relation to practice. Crucially, there was a change from seeing domestic violence as a separate issue from children and child abuse, to seeing it as a possibly central issue for children, and as a part of their abusive experiences. Thus, domestic violence moved from being a peripheral issue, which might sometimes emerge, to being a much more central feature of the team's work. This was reflected in the level of incidence of domestic violence to be seen in the case files. Whereas, in the period prior to the research, one third of cases were identified as involving domestic violence, this rose to two thirds of cases during the research.

Focusing on domestic violence enabled the team to develop a wider contextual framework for the child's experiences. This applied both in those cases where domestic violence was the presenting issue and in those where there were other primary concerns. The impact of living in a context of domestic violence was increasingly taken into account in the work with abused children – both the emotional impact of witnessing violence to (mainly) mothers, and the sexual and/or physical or emotional abuse to the child by the man who was also the domestic violence perpetrator (usually the father or father figure). Overall, there was a move away from the compartmentalising of the different abuses and a focus on the presenting issue to a more integrated, 'holistic' approach where the domestic violence context was taken into account.

As well as providing a wider framework for existing cases, the incorporation of domestic violence meant that a wider range of cases were being accepted for service by the end of the project. In a small number of instances the team were prepared to accept cases where the presenting issue was domestic violence, on the basis that this would constitute emotional abuse of the child and that it might mask other direct abuse. Their concern that this would 'open the floodgates' to an overwhelming increase in referrals was not, however, borne out. The 'domestic violence' referrals remained very small in number, and some were referred on rather than being accepted for service by the team.

Previously the team's work had led them to being concerned that the particular focus which they were expected to adopt had led to a simplistic pathologising of the child as victim, whereby he or she was being perceived in practice as in need of 'rescuing' and needing 'treatment' as if ill. Instead, they were wanting to enable the child to be safe through incorporating and understanding the child's contexts and relationships, and by working in conjunction with the caring adults as well as directly with the child. Having a practice framework that included an understanding of domestic violence was seen to enhance practice and partnership work with parents because it allowed a better understanding of what was going on in many of the cases. There was an increasing tendency to work with mother and child together, or to see mothers, in instances involving domestic violence. By the end of the project the team felt that incorporation of domestic violence was leading to potentially safer and more effective work with women and children.

The project had also led to an increase in the team's interagency links. In particular, the team were in contact with a greater number of voluntary agencies working with women and children experiencing domestic violence. The research had led to participation by the team in a local ACPC conference on domestic violence and one of the team's child protection officers had also become involved in the local domestic violence forum. These developments were seen as positive by the team.

The question remains of how transferable the notions of domestic violence monitoring and reframing would be to other settings and agencies. While it is clear that monitoring is not an accurate means of measuring incidence, it clearly was invaluable in raising awareness, in giving workers permission to ask about domestic violence, and in acting as an 'aide memoire' to do this. Reframing cases was also invaluable to increase awareness and to better understand the dynamics involved in child protection cases involving domestic violence. In all of these positive areas, domestic violence monitoring and the mechanism of reframing would be both transferable and desirable for other agencies who are working with abused children.

# References

Abrahams, C. (1994) *The hidden victims – Children and domestic violence*, London: NCH Action for Children.

Andrews, B. and Brown, G.W. (1988) 'Marital violence in the community: a biographical approach', *British Journal of Psychiatry*, vol 153, pp 305-12.

Armstrong, H. (1994) *ACPC: National Conference: Discussion Report: Annual Reports ACPCs 1992-93*, London: DoH.

Astor, H. (1991) *Position paper on mediation*, Canberra: Office of the Status of Women.

Astor, H. (1994) 'Swimming against the tide: keeping violent men out of mediation', in J. Stubbs (ed) *Women, male violence and the law*, Sydney: Institute of Criminology, Sydney University Law School.

Atkinson, C. (1996) 'Partnership working – supporting those who work with the children of domestic violence', Paper given at the 'Behind Closed Doors' Seminar – 'The effects of Domestic Violence on Children and Vulnerable Young People', Thames Valley.

Ball, M. (1995) *Domestic violence and social care: A report on two conferences held by the Social Services Inspectorate*, London: DoH.

Brandon, M. and Lewis, A. (1996) 'Significant harm and children's experiences of domestic violence', *Child and Family Social Work*, vol 1, no 1, pp 33-42.

Carroll, J. (1994) 'The protection of children exposed to marital violence', *Child Abuse Review*, vol 3, pp 6-14.

Christensen, L. (1990) 'Children's living conditions. An investigation into disregard of care in relation to children and teenagers in families of wife mal-treatment', *Nordisk Psychology*, vol 42, Monograph 31, pp 161-232.

Cleaver, H. and Freeman, P. (1995) *Parental perspectives in cases of suspected child abuse*, London: HMSO.

Dobash, R.E. and Dobash, R.P. (1980) *Violence against wives: A case against the patriarchy*, Sussex: Open Books.

Dobash, R.E. and Dobash, R.P (1984) 'The nature and antecedent of violent events', *British Journal of Criminology*, vol 24, no 3, pp 269-88.

Dobash, R.E. and Dobash, R.P. (1992) *Women, violence and social change*, London: Routledge.

DoH (Department of Health) (1995) *Child protection – Messages from research*, London: DoH.

DoH (1997) Local Authority Circular LAC(97)15 *Family Law Act 1996. Part IV Family Homes and Domestic Violence*, London: DoH.

Edleson, J.L. (1995) 'Mothers and children: understanding the links between woman battering and child abuse', Paper presented at the Strategic Planning Workshop on Violence Against Women, Washington, DC: National Institute of Justice.

Everitt, A., Hardiker, P., Littlewood, J. and Mullender, A. (1992) *Applied research for better practice*, Basingstoke: Macmillan.

Farmer, E. and Owen, M. (1995) *Child protection practice: Private risks and public remedies*, London: HMSO.

Farmer, E. and Pollock, S. (1998: forthcoming) *Substitute care for sexually abused and abusing children*, Chichester: Wiley.

Forman, J. (1995) *Is there a correlation between child sexual abuse and domestic violence? An exploratory study of the links between child sexual abuse and domestic violence in a sample of intrafamilial child sexual abuse cases*, Glasgow: Women's Support Project.

Gibbons, J., Conroy, S. and Bell, C. (1995) *Operating the child protection system: A study of child protection practices in English local authorities*, London: HMSO.

Girdner, L. (1989) 'Dealing with spouse abuse: recommendations for divorce mediators', Academy of Family Mediators, Annual Meeting July.

Glaser, D. and Prior, V. (1997) 'Is the term child protection applicable to emotional abuse?', *Child Abuse Review*, vol 6, pp 315-29.

Goddard, C and Hiller, P. (1993) 'Child sexual abuse: assault in a violent context', *Australian Journal of Social Issues*, vol 28, no 1, pp 20-33.

Hague, G., Malos, E. and Dear, W. (1996) *Multi-agency work and domestic violence: A national study of interagency initiatives*, Bristol: The Policy Press

Hanmer, J. (1989) 'Women and policing in Britain', in J. Hanmer, J. Radford and E. Stanko (eds) *Women, policing and male violence*, London: Routledge.

Hester, M. and Radford, L. (1996) *Domestic violence and child contact arrangements in England and Denmark*, Bristol: The Policy Press.

Hester, M., Pearson, C. and Harwin, N. (1998) *Making an impact. Children and domestic violence. A reader*, London: Barnardos in association with DoH.

Hester, M., Pearson, C. and Radford, L. (1997) *Domestic violence: A national survey of court welfare and voluntary sector mediation practice*, Bristol: The Policy Press.

Home Office, DoH, DES, and Welsh Office (1991) *Working together under the Children Act 1989: A guide to arrangements for inter-agency co-operation for the protection of children from abuse*, London: HMSO.

Humphreys, C. (1997) *Case planning issues where domestic violence occurs in the context of child protection*, Coventry: University of Warwick.

Jaffe, P., Wolfe, D.A. and Wilson, S.K. (1990) *Children of battered women*, California: Sage.

James, G. (1994) *Study of working together Part 8 Reports*, London: DoH.

Kelly, L. (1988) *Surviving sexual violence*, Cambridge: Polity Press.

Kelly, L. (1994) 'The interconnectedness of domestic violence and child abuse: challenges for research, policy and practice', in A. Mullender and R. Morley (eds) *Children living with domestic violence*, London: Whiting and Birch.

Kelly, L. and Radford, J. (1996) 'Nothing really happened: the invalidation of women's expression of sexual violence', in M. Hester, L. Kelly and J. Radford (eds) *Women, violence and male power*, Birmingham: Open University Press.

Kolbo, J., Blakely, E.H. and Engleman, D. (1996) 'Children who witness domestic violence: a review of empirical literature', *Journal of Interpersonal Violence*, vol 11, no 2, pp 281-93.

London Borough of Hackney (1993) *The links between domestic violence and child abuse: Developing services*, London: Hackney Council Press and Publicity Team

Magana, H. and Taylor, N. (1993) 'Child custody mediation and spouse abuse: a descriptive study of a protocol', *Family and Conciliation Courts Review*, vol 31, no 1, pp 50-64.

May, T. (1997) *Social research: issues, methods and process*, 2nd edn, Buckingham: Open University Press.

Maynard, M. (1985) 'The response of social workers to domestic violence', in J. Pahl (ed) Private violence and public policy, London: Routledge.

McGee, C. (forthcoming) *Children's and mother's experiences of child protection following domestic violence*, London: NSPCC.

Mullender, A. and Morley, R. (eds) (1994) *Children living with domestic violence: Putting men's abuse of women on the child care agenda*, London: Whiting and Birch.

O'Hagan, K. and Dillenburger, K. (1995) *Abuse of women within childcare work*, Buckingham: Open University Press.

O'Hara, M. (1994) 'Child deaths in the context of domestic violence: implications for professional practice', in A. Mullender and R. Morley (eds) *Children living with domestic violence: Putting men's abuse of women on the childcare agenda*, London: Whiting and Birch.

Roaf, C. and Lloyd, C. (1995) 'Multi-agency work with young people in difficulty', *Social Care Research*, no 68, Joseph Rowntree Foundation.

Saunders, A. with Epstein, C., Keep, G. and Debbonaire, T. (1995) *It hurts me too: children's experiences of domestic violence and refuge life*, Bristol: WAFE/Childline/NISW.

Shakespeare, P., Atkinson, T. and French, S. (eds) (1993) *Reflecting on research practice*, Buckingham: Open University Press.

Stark, E. and Flitcraft, A.H. (1988) 'Women and children at risk: a feminist perspective on child abuse', *International Journal of Health Studies*, vol 18, no 1, pp 97-119.

# Appendix A: Methodology

As outlined in Chapter 1, the project was carried out in close cooperation between the researchers and the NSPCC team, and a monitoring scheme for domestic violence was devised. To ascertain and chart any changes in the practice of the team a multi-method approach was adopted, including interviews with individuals and the whole team, analysis of case files and monitoring forms, and some observation of practice.

## The monitoring form

After discussions with the team, and building on our previous work (Hester and Radford, 1996; Hester et al, 1997), a system was developed for monitoring domestic violence across all aspects of the team's work. It was decided to use a multi-stage method of monitoring where workers would use a simple monitoring form with all service users at all stages of their work, including initial referral and for each separate session held with service users (see Apendix C for monitoring form layout). Service users were informed of the research and asked to participate, but with an understanding that they were under no obligation to do so. Using this multi-stage approach allowed for disclosure of domestic violence at any point of contact between the NSPCC and the service user and made it possible to analyse the nature of disclosure and to identify those cases where disclosure was not appropriate or possible at the first point of contact. The format of the form was devised to be as straightforward as possible, and included questions about whether domestic violence was an issue, who disclosed this, how this information was obtained, what the domestic violence consisted of and whether this had any impact on the child.

A modified version of the form was developed for use in supervision sessions to enable workers to reflect on their practice in terms of domestic violence.

Following the piloting of the monitoring form for a period of six weeks during December 1996 and January 1997, the team and researchers met to assess the approach adopted. It was decided to make slight modifications to the form, but to continue using the multi-stage approach for the main monitoring exercise from mid-February 1997 until the end of January 1998.

## Case files

The researchers were given access to all case files closed during the period of the project and the previous year, that is from 1 August 1995 until 31 January 1998. Files varied in size and content, recording information from a variety of sources and containing different kinds of documentary evidence (see Chapter 4 for details).

Files contained two types of cases: those which were accepted for service by the NSPCC team, and those which concerned requests for information/advice only or were referred on to other services, especially to social services for investigation purposes. The numbers and types of cases in case file periods A and B were as indicated in Table 1 of this Appendix.

Cases were classified according to the most recent referral request. A few of the referred on/ information only cases had previously been accepted for service by the NSPCC, and in these cases the total file was examined for any indications of domestic violence.

Table 1: Number of files examined

|  | Case file period A | Case file period B |
|---|---|---|
| Total | 131 | 136 |
| Accepted for service | 59 | 52 |
| Information/advice referred on | 72 | 84 |

## Interviews

Individual and team interviews were carried out at various stages throughout the process of the research to provide longitudinal data. Three sets of interviews were carried out:

- at the beginning of the project, interviews were held with each team member in order to determine the range of practice approaches used, and to ascertain their experiences of working with service users where domestic violence was an issue;

- a second set of interviews was undertaken with each team member at the end of the pilot monitoring phase;

- a third set after the completion of the main monitoring stage.

All these interviews were semi-structured and lasted from half an hour to one-and-a-half hours, and were taped and transcribed in full.

In addition to this, regular meetings were held between the researchers and the NSPCC team, where either full notes were taken or the meeting taped and transcribed. The aim of these meetings was to reflect on and assess how the scheme was working, including the use of reframing (see Chapter 3), and to look at the apparent impact and implications for practice.

The data from the interviews, from both individuals and the team meetings, provided complex in-depth information regarding the impact on practice resulting from the project's emphasis on domestic violence, as perceived by team members themselves. This included insights into any issues and difficulties which arose, including debates around the definition and identification of domestic violence and implementation of monitoring. In addition the team interviews provided detailed discussion of individual cases where domestic violence was identified by the researchers, focusing in particular on how or whether domestic violence had been incorporated in practice or what impact this might have had on the progress of the case.

## Observation

In order to better understand the work of the team and the various practice approaches used, the researchers undertook some observations, consisting of both direct observation of 'live' work in sessions and looking at videos of recorded sessions. Team members were also consulted about their views regarding the observed examples of practice.

## User evaluation form

It was intended to ascertain the impact for service users of being asked about domestic violence (see Chapter 7). It was therefore decided to modify the NSPCC's existing user evaluation form to incorporate a simple question on how it felt to be asked about domestic violence. This question was included on the user evaluation forms for both adults and children.

# Appendix B: The NSPCC team and their work

**Table 1: Staffing**

| Staff | At start of project August 1996 | Midway June 1997 | At end of project March 1998 |
|---|---|---|---|
| Team manager/supervisor | 1 | 2 part-time | 1 part-time |
| Child protection officers | 2 full-time and 1 part-time | 1 full-time and 1 part-time | 1 full-time and 1 part-time |
| Therapist | 1 half-time | 1 half-time | 1 half-time |
| Admin/secretarial | 2 full-time | 2 full-time | 1 full-time and 1 part-time |
| Student on placement | 1 | 3 | 0 |

**Table 2: Action by team (during main case file research period)**

| Action by team | Case file period A (total=131) | Case file period B (total=136) |
|---|---|---|
| Accepted for service | 59 (45.0%) | 52 (38.2%) |
| Referred out | 53 (40.5%) | 44 (32.4%) |
| No further action | 19 (14.5%) | 40 (29.4%) |

**Table 3: Type of work accepted for service compared to all requests (during main case file research period) as known**

| Type of work | Requests for service in case file period A | Work accepted in case file period A | Requests for service in case file period B | Work accepted in case file period B |
|---|---|---|---|---|
| Counselling | 40 (30.5%) | 39 (66.1) | 53 (39%) | 38 (73.1%) |
| Treatment/recovery | 7 (5.3%) | 7 (11.9%) | 6 (4.4%) | 6 (11.5%) |
| Assessment | 8 (6.1%) | 5 (8.5%) | 2 (1.5%) | 0 |
| Investigation | 41 (31.3%) | 3 (5.1%) | 48 (35.3%) | 1 (1.9%) |
| Information | 13 (9.9%) | 2 (3.4%) | 8 (5.9%) | 4 (7.7%) |
| Consultation | 2 (1.5%) | 2 (3.4%) | 1 (0.7%) | 1 (1.9%) |
| Prevention | 3 (2.3%) | 1 (1.7%) | 2 (1.5%) | 2 (3.8%) |
| Totals | 131 | 59 | 136 | 52 |

**Table 4: Main concern recorded (during main case file research period)**

| Type of work | Requests for service in case file period A | Accepted for service cases in case file period A | Requests for service in case file period B | Accepted for service cases in case file period B |
|---|---|---|---|---|
| Sexual abuse | 62 (47.3%) | 44 (74.6%) | 63 (46.3%) | 39 (75%) |
| Physical abuse | 29 (22.1%) | 8 (13.6%) | 27 (19.9%) | 4 (7.7%) |
| Emotional abuse | 3 (2.3%) | 0 | 12 (8.8%) | 4 (7.7%) |
| Neglect | 12 (9.2%) | 0 | 11 (8.1%) | 0 |
| Not known | 4 (3.1%) | 2 (3.4%) | 3 (2.2%) | 1 (1.9%) |
| Other | 21 (16%) | 5 (8.5%) | 20 (14.7%) | 4 (7.7%) |
| Totals | 131 | 59 | 136 | 52 |

Only one form of abuse was recorded as the presenting issue for the child concerned but, in reality, service users were likely to have experienced more than one form of abusive behaviour from the same perpetrator (or from several). However, as the staff could only record *one* main concern on their records this somewhat simplified the picture of the service users' experiences of abuse. In relation to practice the staff often found this simplified picture frustrating.

**Table 5: Where requests for service originate, by type of abuse for case file period A**

| | Child | Parent/carer | Relative | Public | Social services department | Other official |
|---|---|---|---|---|---|---|
| Sexual abuse | | 24 | 1 | 7 | 19 | 11 |
| Physical abuse | 4 | 1 | 3 | 11 | 6 | 4 |
| Emotional abuse | | 1 | | 2 | | |
| Neglect | | | 1 | 10 | | |
| Not known | | 1 | | | 1 | 2 |
| Other | 3 | 6 | | 5 | 2 | 5 |
| Totals | 7 | 33 | 5 | 35 | 28 | 22 |

**Table 6: Where requests for service originate, by type of abuse for case file period B**

| | Child | Parent/carer | Relative | Public | Social services department | Other official |
|---|---|---|---|---|---|---|
| Sexual abuse | 1 | 20 | 1 | 6 | 16 | 17 |
| Physical abuse | 4 | 2 | 2 | 12 | 2 | 5 |
| Emotional abuse | | 5 | | 4 | 1 | 2 |
| Neglect | | 1 | | 9 | | 1 |
| Not known | | | | 1 | 1 | 1 |
| Other | | 9 | 2 | 4 | 4 | 1 |
| Totals | 5 | 37 | 5 | 36 | 24 | 27 |

Table 7: Children's gender (where known)

|  | Case file period A | Case file period B |
|---|---|---|
| Girls (total requests) | 95 (59.4%) | 10 (57.4%) |
| Boys (total requests) | 65 (40.6%) | 80 (42.6%) |
| Total children (requests) | 160 | 188 |
| Girls (accepted for service) | 34 (54.8%) | 49 (70.0%) |
| Boys (accepted for service) | 28 (45.2%) | 21 (30.0%) |
| Total children (accepted) | 62 | 70 |

Table 8: The number of mothers and fathers who were classed as requesting a service, or as service users

|  | Case file period A | | Case file period B | |
|---|---|---|---|---|
|  | Of total requested (n=131) | Of accepted for service (n=59) | Of total requested (n=136) | Of accepted for service (n=52) |
| Mothers | 48.9% (n=64) | 52.5% (n=31) | 61% (n=83) | 69.2% (n=36) |
| Fathers | 19.1% (n=25) | 15.3% (n=9) | 14% (n=19) | 3.8% (n=2) |

These figures appear to reflect the continuing attitudes and realities about child welfare being the responsibility of the mother (see Hester et al, 1998), and also the fact that in some cases the fathers were the perpetrators of the abuse and the reason the NSPCC service was required. The higher proportion of fathers in the total sample compared to those accepted for service may also be explained by the practice adopted by some NSPCC staff of classing all members of the family as service users in any investigation request cases, which were largely referred on to social services.

# Appendix C: Domestic violence monitoring form

Date _____ File Number _____

DOMESTIC VIOLENCE MONITORING FORM – CLIENT'S PERSPECTIVE

<u>Every</u> time a white (Referral) form or a blue (Request for service) form or report sheets are filled out, answer the following questions.

1. Does the situation/case involve domestic violence – ie, physical, sexual, psychological, verbal, financial or other violence or abuse used by one adult against his/her partner?

   YES ☐      NO ☐      NOT ASKED/INAPPROPRIATE TO ASK ☐

2. If YES, did it involve:

   physical violence ☐

   sexual assault/abuse ☐

   psychological abuse ☐

   emotional abuse ☐

   verbal abuse ☐

   threats to kill ☐

   financial abuse ☐

   other – give details ☐
   (eg, involving religion, isolation)

3. Did this violence/abuse affect the child(ren)?

   Detail:

   DON'T KNOW ☐

4. How did you find out about the domestic violence?

   Client (adult abuser) mentioned it ☐

   Client (adult abused) mentioned it ☐

   Client (child) mentioned it ☐

   Referrer mentioned it ☐

   Because you asked ☐